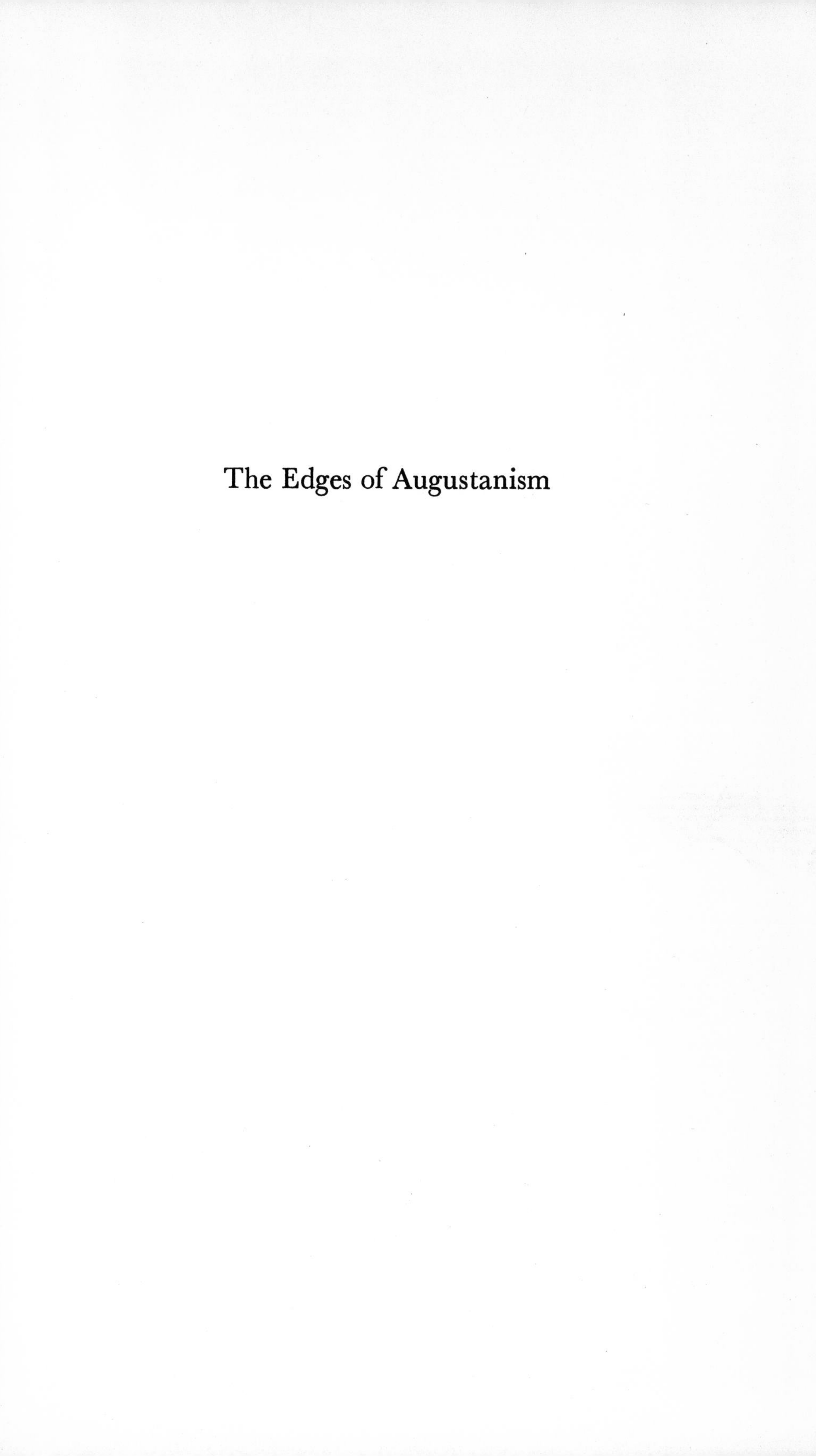

The Edges of Augustanism

ARCHIVES INTERNATIONALES D'HISTOIRE DES IDEES

INTERNATIONAL ARCHIVES OF THE HISTORY OF IDEAS

53

JOHN HOYLES

The Edges of Augustanism

The Aesthetics of Spirituality in Thomas Ken, John Byrom and William Law

The Edges of Augustanism

The Aesthetics of Spirituality in Thomas Ken, John Byrom and William Law

by

JOHN HOYLES

MARTINUS NIJHOFF / THE HAGUE / 1972

ISBN 90 247 1317 X

PRINTED IN THE NETHERLANDS

For Yanik and Dominique

ACKNOWLEDGMENTS

I am particularly grateful to Professor R. L. Brett of Hull and to Professor Knud Sorensen of Aarhus for their generous encouragement and for the assiduous attention with which they have scrutinised drafts of this book.

TABLE OF CONTENTS

INTRODUCTION

It has recently been argued that the 18th century can no longer be seen as gripped in the strait-jacket of Augustanism and Neoclassicism.[1] Such labels are seen as doing less than justice to the rich variety of individual talents and intellectual trends which collectively constitute 18th century culture. While welcoming the interment of the long-standing myth of the peace of the Augustans, there seems little point in placing an interdict on labels which, willy-nilly, have stuck. In economic, social and ecclesiastical terms there is an age between 1689 and 1789 whose homogeneity is reflected in its cultural products. There is a mainstream which the strength and variety of counter-currents and cross-currents corroborate rather than disintegrate. It is the purpose of this study to reveal some aspects of this mainstream by examining certain cross-currents which overlap its edges. Hence the choice of Thomas Ken (1637–1711), John Byrom (1692–1763) and William Law (1686–1761).

Ken was excluded from his bishopric in 1689 and Law and Byrom's fruitful friendship began in 1729. These are dates when crises in the lives of individuals coincide with crises in the cultural and social life of the body politic. Thus Ken's verse inevitably reflects the spirit of of the 1690s, a decade during which the recent dynastic upheaval ushered in the social and economic infrastructure on which Augustanism could be erected. Ken did not die until 1711, by which time Byrom was an undergraduate and Law a Fellow of Emmanuel. The via media of Augustanism further consolidated itself by withstanding the dynastic crisis of 1715, the year in which Law, like Ken before him, became a non-juror. The work of Byrom and Law reflects the spirit of the 1730s, the last decade before the rise of Evangelicalism

[1] See Donald Greene, "Augustinianism and Empiricism: a Note on 18th Century English Intellectual History," *18th Century Studies*, I (1967), 33–68.

began to make inroads into the cultural habits and institutions of the Augustan hegemony. The appearance of the Wesleys' hymns in 1739 marks a new watershed, though Augustanism was by then sufficiently well-entrenched to do battle until the end of the century.

It is within this broad but specific framework that the edges of Augustanism may be defined and examined. The kind of spirituality which the Augustan settlement sought to eliminate cannot be dissociated from a certain kind of aesthetic, which in Ken relates to the survival of the Metaphysical tradition and in Byrom and Law to the rise of Romanticism. In both cases it might be instructive to view the aesthetics of spirituality against the edges of Augustanism as well as against the counter-currents with which they are more naturally associated. In this perspective Ken, Byrom and Law are as much representatives of an exuberant and heterogeneous Augustan age, as iconoclastic relics and prophets.[2]

If Neoclassicism is a central feature of Augustanism, without having to be coextensive with it, then Ken, Byrom and Law are by no means total outsiders. Thus Ken's satiric couplets fit quite nicely into Neoclassical development between Dryden and Pope, and Law's prose, with its eloquent clarity, is comparable to that of Berkeley and Gibbon. As for Byrom, if we view him as a minor poet, independent of Law, he appears as an impeccably neoclassical Augustan. An inventor of a shorthand method, Byrom was interested in developing John Wilkins's scheme for establishing a universal character and language.[3] His "Art of English Poetry" is a model of orthodox neoclassical theory, with its formulae on wit and judgment, and with its taste for verse which aspires to the condition of prose. Byrom merely adds a plea for verse which would be subject to the precision and brevity of his shorthand method.[4]

It is nevertheless for their strategic positions at the two ends of the Augustan age that Ken, Byrom and Law stand out. Ken, like Marvell before him, tells us something of the frontiers between Metaphysical and Augustan, and Byrom and Law point unequivocally towards Coleridge. In this perspective their lyricism and thought, however

[2] Cf. Donald Greene's new look at the Augustan Age, *The Age of Exuberance* (New York: Random House, 1970).

[3] See Mr Windham to J. Byrom, 18 December 1737, in John Byrom, *Private Journal and Literary Remains*, ed. Richard Parkinson (2 vols., issued in 4 parts; "Chetham Society Remains", Vols. 32, 34, 40, 44; Manchester: Chetham Society, 1854–7), II, 191.

[4] "An Epistle to a Friend on the Art of English Poetry," esp. lines 81–94, in John Byrom, *Poems*, ed. A. W. Ward (3 vols., issued in 5 parts; "Chetham Society Remains, New Series," Vols. 29, 30, 34, 35, 70; Manchester: Chetham Society, 1894–1912), I, 399.

meagre or eccentric by conventional aesthetic or philosophical criteria, stand out in sharp relief against the spirit of their age. At first they appear to be anachronisms, but Law's militant and systematic thought has many advanced features which belie its surface obscurantism, and even Ken provides certain hints which Newman could use in his critique of Augustanism.

The limitations of Ken, Byrom and Law are clear enough for all to see. Some of these may be put down to the natural awkwardness of men who were in large measure at odds with the prevailing tendencies of their age. Thus much of Ken's cumbrous artificiality reflects the impact which Neoclassicism made on the Metaphysical tradition. This artificiality is paralleled in the work of Cowley, Cleveland and the early Dryden. It corresponds to a split in the intellectual consciousness which Restoration court-culture accentuated. Herbert's verse conspicuously does not suffer from this split. But then Herbert died well before the civil wars got going. And there is an additional personal factor to be taken into consideration. Herbert retired from court at the relatively early age of 34, whereas Ken, thrust into the world of ecclesiastical politics and royal mistresses, withdrew under duress to ponder the incongruity of his career at the ripe old age of 52.

The awkwardness and cumbrous artificiality of Byrom and Law are in retrospect less evident. Byrom's genial bonhomie ensured that he enjoyed mulling over the fashionable topics which rose to the surface of coffee-house chat. In this sense he was positively Augustan. His contact with the eccentric Law, isolated in the anti-Augustan atmosphere of King's Cliffe, was his lifeline to another world.[5] The nature of this world is perhaps best defined by Coleridge who, after studying the works of two centuries of scientific progress and intellectual enlightenment, declared:

> There exist folios on the human understanding, and the nature of man, which would have a far juster claim to their high rank and celebrity, if in the whole huge volume there could be found as much fulness of heart and intellect, as burst forth in many a simple page of George Fox, Jacob Behmen, and even of Behmen's commentator, the pious and fervid William Law... The writings of these mystics acted in no slight degree to prevent my mind from being imprisoned within the outline of any single dogmatic system. They contributed to keep alive the heart in the head; gave me an indistinct, yet stirring and working presentiment, that all the products of the mere reflective faculty partook of death, and were as the rattling twigs and sprays

[5] King's Cliffe is the Northamptonshire village, six miles south of Stamford, where Law lived from 1740 until his death.

in winter, into which a sap was yet to be propelled from some root to which I had not penetrated, if they were to afford my soul either food or shelter.[6]

Once again, from the perspective implied in the sequence of Boehme, Fox, Law and Coleridge, it is perhaps too easy to characterise Augustanism as a strait-jacket within which the human spirit could not for long be confined. This is not a conclusion which is very profitable except to those who wish to ignore the significance of 18th century culture. The facts are a little more complicated and, need we say, interesting.

Law may have been, as Leslie Stephen suggests in a chapter entitled "The Religious Reaction," " a perfect incarnation of the counteracting forces which were gradually stirring beneath the surface of society."[7] He was also in many ways as typical and original a product of the 18th century as Edward Gibbon whose father he tutored. Endowed with a "sensitiveness to logic ... as marked as his sensitiveness to conscience," and with a strength and clarity of reason tending naturally to the "form of a *reductio ad absurdam*,"[8] Law embodies, with Gibbon and Hume, one of the redeeming features of the 18th century mind. Whether one views these writers as extremists operating a pincer movement on an impoverished Augustan via media, or as the finest flower of Augustanism, is in the last resort a relatively academic question.

Coleridge's view of Law as "pious and fervid" is not without justice. But it underestimates two aspects of Law's thought which are of interest to the modern reader. The first is the way in which Law belongs to the line Pascal-Kierkegaard as a forerunner of existentialist theology. His efforts at theological renewal were eclipsed by the more popular and traditional ideas preached by John Wesley, but are now bearing strange fruit in the age of the "death of God."

The second feature of Law's thought which Coleridge less excusably underestimated concerns the relationship between philosophy and aesthetics. Noone did more than Coleridge to overhaul this relationship. He was among the first to point out that aesthetics was no mere question of taste but depended on a philosophical infrastructure. Law of course was not concerned with aesthetics, but this thought and spirituality are fraught with more far-reaching implications than are

[6] S. T. Coleridge, *Biographia Literaria*, ed. Arthur Symons (London: J. M. Dent, 1906), Chapter 9, pp. 75–6.

[7] Leslie Stephen, *History of English Thought in the 18th Century* (2 vols.; London: Rupert Hart-Davis, 1962), II, 331.

[8] *Ibid.*, II, 336, 341.

the ostensibly aesthetic investigations conducted by his contemporaries, the preromantics. Indeed Law's contribution in this respect owed much to the fact that he was insulated from the current trends.

In the following pages these issues are pursued in a more pragmatic fashion and in the process the reader may decide for himself how far new contradictions are left unattended and how far the aesthetics of spirituality cast light on the edges of Augustanism.

PART ONE

THOMAS KEN

CHAPTER ONE

THE CRITICAL HERITAGE

Thomas Ken, born in 1637, was a contemporary of Traherne (b.1637) and Dryden (b.1631). This generation, coming to age just before the Restoration, is situated at a strategic moment in English cultural history. The old habits of intellectual liberty and aesthetic licence have yet to be controlled and refined under the new dispensation of Anglican and Neoclassical settlement. While Dryden heroically welcomed the new dispensation, contributing largely to its definition, and while Traherne sublimated the old freedoms and fancies into a striking, if anachronistic, personal vision, Ken did a bit of both. Ken is equally at home writing a Caroline devotional lyric or turning his hand to Restoration Hudibrastic satire. One edge of Augustanism can thus be examined in his work.

Ken might not have written any verse were it not for the 1688 Revolution which made of him a non-juror, emphasised his links with the pre-latitudinarian generation of Caroline lyricists, and gave him time to compose his vast rambling epics. As it is, he turned out four volumes of verse which show him to be as conversant with the poetic mode of Dryden as with that of George Herbert.[1] Such a phenomenon invites investigation, especially since, according to Grierson, "the central heat" of Metaphysical poetry "died down" with the advent of Cowley who himself died in 1667.[2] Most critics have followed Grierson in the view that by 1667 "the long wrestle between reason and imagination has ended in the victory of reason, good sense."[3] The question therefore arises whether Ken's verse, almost certainly

[1] Thomas Ken, *Works*, ed. William Hawkins (4 vols.; London: V. Wyat, 1721). These are the poetical works. Separate prose works were published during his lifetime and posthumously.

[2] H. J. C. Grierson, *Metaphysical Lyrics and Poems of the 17th Century: Donne to Butler* (Oxford: Clarendon Press, 1921), p. lvi. See also Geoffrey Walton, *Metaphysical to Augustan: Studies in Tone and Sensibility in the 17th Century* (London: Bowes and Bowes, 1955), p. 51.

[3] Grierson, p. lvi.

written after 1690,[4] constitutes an eccentric relic, or whether it reveals anything about the relationship between Metaphysical and Augustan poetic modes.

It was T. S. Eliot's contention that the central tradition of Metaphysical poetry was marked by a "tough reasonableness beneath the slight lyric grace."[5] It is usually held that the work of Herbert and Marvell lives up to this formula, and it may be that in Ken the split is all too open between the satiric mode ("tough reasonableness") and the pietistic effusions to which the "slight lyric grace" has degenerated. But then it should be remembered that Marvell's lyrics belong to a pre-Restoration age, and that after the Restoration Marvell's "tough reasonableness" finds expression in prose and verse not particularly distinguished for its "slight lyric grace." Thus the nature of Ken's verse remains teazingly instructive.

Criticism, or even notice, of Ken's verse is almost non-existent. He has been valued by the public schools for the hymns and manuals of devotion he composed for the boys of Winchester, and by the Oxford Movement for his churchmanship.[6] He was evidently an eloquent and courageous preacher, with a prose style worthy of a pre-latitudinarian divine. But, from their publication in 1721, his poetical works have received as little attention as the vast religious epics of Samuel Wesley.[7] If he was read at all, it was for his opinions as a non-juring high-churchman. One of his 18th century admirers was the extreme high-flyer, Thomas Gent (1693–1778), who in "The Holy Life and Death of St Winifred" (1743), refers to King Edmund as

> High praised by God-like Ken
> The most seraphic of all mortal men.[8]

[4] In *A Short Account of T. Ken D.D.* (London: J. Wyat, 1713), p. 24, William Hawkins represents Ken as writing one of his epics on the return voyage from Tangier in 1684. Cf. Margaret Cropper, *Flame Touches Flame* (London: Longmans Green, 1949), p. 200. Ken may well have begun an epic during the Tangier voyage, but internal evidence suggests that the bulk of his verse was written after his ejection from Wells.

[5] T. S. Eliot, *Selected Essays* (London: Faber and Faber, 1934), p. 293.

[6] Ken's reputation for saintliness existed in his own lifetime. Dryden's description of the poor parson in his translation of Chaucer (1700) was apparently a tribute to Ken. In *Tracts for the Times*, No. 75 (1836), Newman proposed a breviary for the use of Anglicans with March 21st as Bishop Ken's day. In 1839 Disraeli noted in a letter: "M. Rion . . . says that Bishop Ken was the Fénelon of England, and that the Oxford Tracts are a mere revival of his works. It is the non-jurors again." E. H. Plumptre, *The Life of Thomas Ken, Bishop of Bath and Wells* (2 vols.; London: W. Isbister, 1888), II, 258–9, 273–4.

[7] Samuel Wesley, the Elder (1662–1735), author of *The Life of our Blessed Lord and Saviour Jesus Christ. An Heroic Poem* (1693) in ten books, and of *The History of the Old and New Testament Attempted in Verse* (1704–15).

[8] Quoted in H. N. Fairchild, *Religious Trends in English Poetry* (5 vols.; New York: Columbia University Press, 1939–62), I, 309. Cf. Walter Harte (1709–74) who referred iriadmngly to the "seraphic Ken." *Ibid.*, II, 63.

Ken's most recent biographer, H. A. L. Rice, confines himself to noticing that "Edmund" is "written in the manner of Cowley, ... fashioned in the artificial style then in vogue," and that this style may contain "polish, grace and wit in Cowley, Dryden etc.," but becomes inevitably "pedestrian and banal in the hands of less skilful practitioners."[9] This is short shrift, however much justice it does to one aspect of Ken's verse.

Between the uncritical hero-worship of Gent and the scant lip-service of Rice, 19th century criticism, Keble excepted, is disappointingly brief. Bowles found Ken's poetry repugnant in the extreme, disliked his "discordant imagery," his "vulgarity of language" and his "wretched execution," placed him "far below Blackmore," and accused him of the unforgiveable sin of using the "language of human passions in speaking of divine and spiritual objects,"[10] Anderdon found his "grotesque flights beyond the limits of taste," though there were "couplets here and there, so terse and pointed as to remind us of Pope."[11] And Alexander Knox was content to give Ken his place in the development of the English hymn.[12] Ampler paragraphs of more considered appreciation do not exist outside the pages of Keble in the 19th century and Fairchild in the 20th century.

Keble's appreciation is qualified. As he says, "the simple and touching devoutness of many of Bishop Ken's lyrical effusions has been unregarded, because of the ungraceful contrivances and heavy movement of his narrative." Keble regrets that Ken had "so little confidence in the power of simplicity and condescended so largely to the laborious refinements of the profane muse."[13] Yet he considers Ken worthy of notice as a lyricist as well as a high-church martyr.[14] Referring to the "splendid and gorgeous strains" and to the "sense

[9] H. A. L. Rice, *Thomas Ken: Bishop and Non-Juror* (London: Society for the Propagation of Christian Knowledge, 1958), p. 182.

[10] Bowles, *Life of Ken* (1830), II, 290–300. Quoted in Plumptre, II, 232–3.

[11] J. L. Anderdon, *The Life of Thomas Ken. By a Layman* (2nd ed. revised and enlarged; London, 1854), p. 747. Cf. Bishop William Alexander's "Sermon in Wells Cathedral" (1885), quoted in Plumptre, II, 288: "The heroic couplets occasionally remind us that we are between the richness of Dryden and the compression of Pope."

[12] Alexander Knox, *Remains*, III, 226, quoted in Plumptre, II, 265–6: "A comparison of the hymns of Doddridge, Watts, Ken and Wesley would show that Doddridge rises above Watts from having caught the spirit of Ken; and Wesley is deep and interior from having added to the Chrysostomian piety of Ken the experimental part of St Augustine. Watts is a pure Calvinist; Ken is as pure a Chrysostomian. Doddridge is induced to blend both, and the effect is valuable and interesting; Wesley advances this union."

[13] John Keble, "Sacred Poetry," *The Quarterly Review*, XXXII (1825), 217.

[14] Keble planned to produce a selection of Ken's writings including "some choice bits of his poetry." See Plumptre, II, 267.

of decay" in the devotional verse of the Romanists, he writes:

A feeling of this kind, joined to the effect of distressing languour and sickness, may be discerned occasionally in the writings of Bishop Ken; though he was far indeed from being a Romanist. We shall hardly find in all ecclesiastical history, a greener spot than the later years of this courageous and affectionate pastor; persecuted alternately by both parties, and driven from his station in his declining age; yet singing on, with unabated cheerfulness, to the last.[15]

Fairchild offers a similar picture, rightly placing Ken's lyricism in its historical context as a rare example of transitional talent neither Metaphysical nor preromantic:

The historian of serious lyrical poetry must traverse a desert lying between the 17th century singers and the 18th century precursors of the great Romantic lyricists. Yet there are a few relatively green oases amidst the sands – Ken, Norris, Mrs Rowe, Watts... In them the song of inward feeling, albeit precariously and fitfully, continues to exist.[16]

But Fairchild too puts his finger on Ken's fundamental weakness: the contrived artificiality of much of his verse. Where Keble saw this weakness arising from a contamination of the sacred by the profane, Fairchild sees it as a manifestation of a derivative, unassimilated Metaphysical style:

The age gave him too little of the peace which his gentle nature needed, and often forced him to preach and argue in verse. At such times he tends to be flat and verbose. Without possessing a truly Metaphysical genius, he sometimes indulges in conceits which are quaintly rather than movingly outlandish. He is too fond of fussy allegorical devices and of strange adjectives like "cotrine," "antesolar," "salvifick," and "chaolick"... In general he writes like a contemporary of Phineas Fletcher who has lived on into times which nourish neither his thought nor his art.[17]

If both critics admire the man, and sympathise with the difficult circumstances of his ecclesiastical career, they are also agreed in their qualified appreciation of the poet. Keble's final assessment runs as follows:

His poems are not popular, nor, probably, ever will be; ... but whoever in earnest loves his three well-known hymns, and knows how to value such unaffected strains of poetical devotion, will find his account, in turning over his four volumes, half narrative and half lyric, and all avowedly on

[15] Keble, p. 230.
[16] Fairchild, I, 209.
[17] *Ibid.*, I, 105.

sacred subjects: the narrative often cumbrous, and the lyric verse not seldom languid and redundant: yet all breathing such an angelic spirit, interspersed with such pure and bright touches of poetry, that such a reader as we have supposed will scarcely find it in his heart to criticise them.[18]

This critical appreciation constitutes a valid invitation to examine more closely the four volumes of Ken's poetical works.

[18] Keble, p. 231.

CHAPTER TWO

THE RELIGIOUS BACKGROUND

Ken was no philosopher. He was not at home with ideas. Nor did he seek truth with the eagerness of a pioneer or the confidence of a consolidator. In this he reminds us that Augustanism was not a movement of disembodied ideas. Augustanism did not live by intellect alone; it was nourished by the more substantial roots of political and ecclesiastical establishment. Bishop Ken's background is thus relevant to a study of the impact of Augustanism on English poetry. Before we go on to analyse what in his poetry is pure, bright and angelic, and what cumbrous, languid and redundant, and to relate such an analysis to the transition from Metaphysical to Augustan, we should give some account of this background.

Something of the atmosphere of the period can be glimpsed in the lively pamphlets of George Hickes, leader of the militant non-jurors, and John Dunton, Defoe's rival as self-appointed spokesman for the Whig Dissenters. The latitudinarian spirit had not yet blunted the edges of controversy; indeed both Hickes and Dunton accuse their adversaries of being tainted with latitudinarianism, and therefore unprincipled.

Hickes, in his 1695 pamphlet, is attacking Gilbert Burnet as the leading ecclesiastic involved in bringing about the 1688 Revolution; but through him, he aims at the whole latitudinarian movement, whose high-priests had been Wilkins and Tillotson. He begins with a satiric portrait of Burnet, in which the political broadside spills over into a linguistic critique:

No style of any sort of writers, plain or polished, coarse or fine, can please him in any language; be they English or foreigners, Protestants or Papists, divines or lawyers, if they are his adversaries they cannot escape his insolent censure. But if they are friends and partisans, and men of his feather, then their style is exact, neither sinking nor swelling, plain, distinct, short, clear, all of one piece, without superfluity of words, superficial strains of false thoughts, or bold flights; all solid, yet lively, and grave as well as free. The Wilkinses and Tillotsons, that are for the *Liberties of Mankind*, and have *large thoughts* of things, . . . they are all the patterns for the world to follow; but the men of strict principles, *the narrow, the hot, the warm, the angry, and the peevish men*, are unaccurate, and little writers, that understand true eloquence as little, as the *just freedom of human nature.*[1]

Hickes's parallel between linguistic and political activities constitutes a telling polemical point when one remembers that Wilkins and Tillotson were pioneers of language reform as well as leaders of the latitudinarian faction.

John Dunton, in the early years of the 18th century, speaks for the opposing faction when, in an attack on behalf of Whig Dissenters against the notorious Jacobite, Charles Leslie, he writes:

My last undeserved and public enemy is Leslie, the tacking author of that scandalous paper called *The Rehearsal*. This scribbling Levite hath flung a great deal of dirt at me and the present government. . . For his religion, if he have any, it is altogether for liberty of conscience; but, whilst he keeps loose his own, he stickles hard for an Occasional Bill to bind other men's. He would make a bad martyr, and a good traveller: for his conscience is so large, he could never wander out of it; and in Amsterdam, as much as he hates Dissenters, could pass for a stiff Independent.[2]

Ken was living in retirement during this period, and took no part in such heated controversy. He had been a good martyr and a bad traveller, a man of "strict principles" and, in the eyes of the Augustan Enlightenment, one of "the peevish men" without "large thoughts of things." Ken was as close to the non-jurors and the Metaphysical tradition as he was far from the aesthetics and ideology of the Wil-

[1] George Hickes, *Some Discourses upon Dr Burnet and Dr Tillotson occasioned by the late funeral sermon of the former upon the latter* (1695). Quoted in L. G. Locke, *Tillotson, A Study in 17th Century Literature* ("Anglistica," No. 4; Copenhagen: Rosenkilde and Bagger, 1954), p. 63. Hickes (1642–1715) was consecrated non-juring bishop of Thetford in 1694. His *Spirit of Enthusiasm Exorcised* (1680) was praised by Cudworth, More and Whichcote. In addition to editing Thomas à Kempis and Fénelon, he published *The Spirit of Popery speaking out of the Mouths of Phanatical Protestants* (1680) and *An Apology for the New Separation* (1691). *DNB*.

[2] John Dunton, *Life and Errors*, ed. J. B. Nichols (London, 1818), pp. 453, 455. Dunton (1659–1733) was an enterprising bookseller whose many projects included the *Athenian Gazette* (1690–6). Charles Leslie (1650–1722) was a leading non-juror and prolific controversialist. In 1693 he visited St Germain and obtained from the Pretender the *congé d'élire* for the consecration of the non-juring bishops. Few escaped attack from his vitriolic pen; his victims include Burnet (1694), Tillotson and Sherlock (1695), Quakers (1696–1701), Deists and Jews (1698), Dissenters and mixed marriages (1702), Socinians (1708) and Hoadly (1709–11). According to Dr Johnson, Leslie was "the only reasoner among the non-jurors." *DNB*

kinses and Tillotsons of this world. In the eyes of Hickes's ironic persona, and of the Enlightenment, Ken no doubt belonged to that category of "little writers, that understand true eloquence as little as the just freedom of human nature."[3] Unlike the militant Hickes however, Ken removed himself from the cockpit of debate and abuse, and in stately retirement cultivated his own out-of-date conceptions of "true eloquence" and "just freedom."

Ken took no part in the post-1688 controversy, because it was above everything else a political quarrel. Drawn across the stage of English history half way between the age of Andrewes and the age of Hoadly, he was more at home in the former than in the latter. He believed in "eucharistic might,"[4] at a time when, as an Anglican historian has put it, "victories at the polls were more sought after than triumphs of the cross, and Atterbury takes the place of Ken as the typical churchman of his time."[5]

In his early days however, before the political issues were clear, and before the Church of England had felt the full effects of the Restoration settlement as legislated by the Clarendon Code, Ken had launched a bitter broadside against the folly of accommodation and compromise. The fourth section of *Ichabod; or Five Groans of the Church*, a pamphlet published anonymously in 1663, is entitled, "The Church of England's resentment of the 1342 factious ministers that have been lately ordained." Ken sees no point in accommodating time-servers and innate dissenters:

In vain doth authority silence your old adversaries, if you consecrate new ones: in vain do they suppress the former race of Non-conformists, if you raise up a new generation... Shall we perpetuate our miseries and keep up our unhappiness? Must a sad race of Dissenters run parallel with the orthodox succession to the end of the world? ... Alas, to see men Pres-

[3] According to L. G. Locke (p. 115), there is only one conceit in the whole of Tillotson's works, and that one escapes, significantly, in the course of a compliment to King William.

[4] Ken, IV, 97.

[5] H. O. Wakeman, *An Introduction to the History of the Church of England* (1914). Quoted in Fairchild, I, 95. Francis Atterbury (1662–1732), champion of the high-church clergy against the latitudinarians, began associating with Jacobites in 1717 and left England in 1723 as an exile. He was considered to be the ablest preacher of his day and counted Swift, Pope, Newton and Bolingbroke among his friends. Benjamin Hoadly (1676–1761), leader of the low-church divines from 1709 and absentee Bishop of Bangor (1715–21), came under general attack from the high-church clergy in the Bangorian Controversy (1717–20) following the publication of *A Preservative against the Principles and Practices of the Nonjurors both in Church and State* (1716). It was in this heated debate that William Law made his literary début with *Three Letters to the Bishop of Bangor* (1717–19) which has since come to be regarded as the most effective of the many replies to Hoadly. Hoadly was on good terms with Samuel Clarke, to whose refined Arianism he was sympathetic; indeed he professed so low a latitudinarianism as to be almost a Socinian. *DNB*

byterian in the beginning of the war, Independent in the end of it, and now Episcopal. Where shall we stop? ... Alas, is a good living the only creed men have? and preferment their only confession of faith? It was a miracle that St Peter could convert three thousand at one sermon. It is nothing now that his majesty hath converted ten thousand ministers with one glance of his eye.[6]

To Ken, the career of Wilkins, Warden of Wadham under the Commonwealth, married to Cromwell's sister, then preferred to a bishopric under Charles II, must have been an affront.

Wilkins's biographer has called attention to his unorthodox background. His tutor was a certain John Tombes (1603–1676). According to Aubrey, Tombes, active in Oxford as late as 1664, "set up a challenge to maintain 'contra omnes gentes' the Anabaptistical doctrine; but not a man would grapple with him." Aubrey concludes with wry satisfaction that "putting aside his Anabaptistical positions he was conformable enough to the Church of England."[7] Here clearly was one of Ken's "factious ministers," and an illustration of the tolerance which the Clarendon Code was intended to eliminate. In the sober words of Wilkins's biographer,

it is doubtful whether Mr Tombes would now, if he came back, move in Episcopal circles. His career gives us a glimpse into those puzzling times of confusion and cross-purposes, when compromise and toleration coexisted, both in parties and individuals, with bitter fanaticism, more commonly than is supposed, or can be explained.[8]

Ken would no doubt have shared Anthony Wood's view of Wilkins as

a notorious complier with the Presbyterians (from whom he obtained the wardenship of Wadham); with the Independents; and Cromwell himself, by whose favour he did not only get a dispensation to marry (contrary to the College statutes but also (because he had married his sister) Master of Trinity College in Cambridge. From which being ejected at the Restoration, faced about and by his smooth language, insinuating preaching, flatteries, and I know not what, got, among other preferments, the deanery of Ripon; and at length (by the commendation of George Villiers duke of Buckingham, a great favourer of fanatics and atheists) the bishopric of Chester.[9]

[6] Thomas Ken, *The Prose Works*, ed. W. Benham (London: Griffith, Farran, Okeden and Welsh, 1889), pp. 23, 25. *Ichabod* was reprinted anonymously as *Lachrymae Ecclesiarum* (1689) and in Ken's name as *Expostulatoria, or the Complaints of the Church* (1709).

[7] John Aubrey, *Brief Lives*, ed. Andrew Clark (2 vols.; Oxford: Clarendon Press, 1898), II, 259. See also P. A. Wright Henderson, *The Life and Times of John Wilkins* (Edinburgh: W. Blackwood, 1910), p. 32.

[8] Henderson, p. 33. Tombes was in fact befriended by Clarendon at the Restoration. He maintained his Baptist beliefs while communicating as an Anglican. *DNB*

[9] Anthony Wood, *Life and Times*, ed. Andrew Clark (5 vols.; Oxford Historical Society; Oxford: Clarendon Press, 1891–1900), I, 363. Quoted in Henderson, pp. 124–5.

In the diocese of Chester, Wilkins succeeded, by wise and tolerant accommodation, in eliminating the "sad race of Dissenters"; but in the long run, both Ken and Wilkins, though from opposite extremes, were fighting a losing battle, for the Dissenters were there to stay.

After the crisis of 1688 however, the Dissenters came to be accommodated in fact, if not in form, by the widespread practice of occasional conformity; while it was Ken and his party who chose to exclude themselves from the political and ecclesiastical establishment.[10] The political implications of Ken's high-churchmanship are never so apparent as in the 1688 sermon, in which he states the doctrine of non-resistance in terms which show that he places the purity of religious motive above even loyalty to the Stuart dynasty:

> The Children of Israel ... were to subject their persons to the Babylonish government, but not to prostitute their consciences to the Babylonish idolatry... To have then obeyed the king, had not been allegiance, but apostasy. In such cases the true Israelites would always be martyrs, but never rebels: they resolutely chose to obey God, and patiently to suffer the lion's den, the fiery furnace, and the extremity of the king's displeasure.[11]

Thus it was that, under James II, and in the revolutionary days that followed the imprisonment of the bishops, Ken acted always as a martyr, never as a rebel. As he was to write in "Edmund":

> Our Zeal supreme must on Religion wait,
> And next on the prosperity of State.[12]

This favourite argument of the high-church party was to come under fire from the Dissenters, when the bill against occasional conformity was introduced in 1702. Isaac Watts commented:

> A vote decides the blind debate;
> Resolved 'tis of diviner weight
> To save the steeple than the state.[13]

And Defoe, indefatigable to score a party point, linked the bill with the celebrated storm of 1703, in which Wells cathedral was struck by

[10] In 1689 an attempt to accommodate Dissenters failed because of opposition from the high-church country clergy. See L. G. Locke, p. 81. John Dunton celebrates the virtual accommodation which came into being after the 1688 Revolution in an address entitled "To the Dissenting Clergy: but more especially to those who lately took or accepted the degree of D.D. in the Scottish Universities; in which is proved this paradox, that Protestant Churchmen and such as dissent from it, are members of the same Church." Dunton, p. 695.

[11] Ken, *Prose Works*, p. 106.

[12] Ken, II, 198.

[13] Isaac Watts, "To David Polhill Esq." (1702), in *Works*, ed. D. Jennings and P. Doddridge (6 vols.; London, 1753), II, 403.

lightning; he calls it

> a high-church storm,
> Sent out the nation to reform;
> But the emblem left the moral in the lurch,
> For 't blew the steeple down upon the church.
> From whence we now inform the people,
> The danger of the church is from the steeple.
> And we've had many a bitter stroke,
> From pinnacle and weather-cock;
> From whence the learned do relate,
> That to secure the church and state,
> The time will come when all the town
> To save the church, will pull the steeple down.[14]

The doggerel suits the transparent allegory, and wittily voices the Whig attitude towards the high-church party. Defoe's prophecy came true, but the high-flyers did not lightly surrender their steeple.

The case for the steeple, and against occasional conformity, was put obliquely but with all the persuasive force of common sense by the two greatest prose-writers of the age of Queen Anne. Berkeley equates occasional conformity with deism and libertinism, when he makes his minute philosopher, Lysicles, declaim with ironical plausibility:

> We are too wise to think there is anything sacred either in king or constitution, or indeed in anything else. A man of sense may perhaps seem to pay an occasional regard to this prince; but his is no more at bottom than what he pays to God, when he kneels at the sacrament to qualify himself for an office.[15]

Berkeley's inference is clear; he who dissents in religion is liable to dissent in politics. Swift's position is less clear but more incisive. In his *Project for the Advancement of Religion, and the Reformation of Manners* (1709), he makes havoc of the whole Occasional Conformity controversy, with an irony that bites in all directions at once. It may be thought, he writes,

> that the making religion a necessary step to interest and favour, might increase hypocrisy among us: and I readily believe it would. But if one in twenty should be brought over to true piety by this, or the like methods, and the other nineteen be only hypocrites, the advantage would still be great. Besides, hypocrisy is much more eligible than open infidelity and vice... And, I believe, it is often with religion as it is with love; which, by much dissembling, at last grows real.[16]

14 Daniel Defoe, "The Storm" (1703). Quoted in Fairchild, I, 73–4.
15 George Berkeley, *Alciphron*, ed. T. E. Jessop (London: T. Nelson, 1950), p. 52.
16 Jonathan Swift, *Works*, ed. H. Davis (14 vols.; Oxford: Blackwell, 1939–62), II, 56–7.

Swift carries the art of plausibility so far that he identifies himself with his butt, and occasional conformity with common sense. But does the reader imagine Swift to be "so weak" as "to stand up in the defence of real Christianity?"

Swift and Berkeley of course had a vested interest in the steeple and total conformity, but eventually England weathered the "high-church storm." It turned out that Watts and Defoe, with their verse doggerel, were on the winning side, while Swift and Berkeley had to be content with the consolation of their golden prose. In the meteorological storm however, Ken was spared; it was his latitudinarian usurper at Wells who perished. And Lady Winchilsea, moved like Defoe by the storm into verse, pointed a very different moral in this pretty tribute to Ken:

> O Wells! Thy Bishop's mansion we lament
> So tragical the fall, so dire the event!
> But let no daring thought presume
> To point a cause for that oppressive doom.
> Yet, strictly pious Ken! hadst thou been there,
> This fate, we think, had not become thy share;
> Nor had that awful fabric bowed,
> Sliding from its loosened bands;
> Not yielding timbers been allowed
> To crush thy ever-lifted hands,
> Or interrupt thy prayer.[17]

Ken's deliverance was even more dramatic than Lady Winchilsea knew.[18] But at least his high-churchmanship did not go unacknowledged by one who was herself prominent at Longleat.[19]

The death of Kidder, who had replaced Ken at Bath and Wells after the 1688 revolution, led Queen Anne to offer the see back to its original occupant; but Ken was an old man, and, following the appointment of Hooper of whom he approved, he no longer signed

[17] Anne Finch, Countess of Winchilsea, "A Pindaric Poem. Upon the Hurricane in November 1703," lines 96–106, in *Poems*, ed. Myra Reynolds (Chicago: University Press, 1903), pp. 255–6. Richard Kidder (1633–1703) was consecrated Bishop of Bath and Wells in 1691. His diocese maintained a sullen hostility towards him, accusing him in particular of ordaining Dissenters without due attention to their orthodoxy. *DNB.* He and his wife were killed when the palace chimneys were struck by lightning on the 27th of November. According to Plumptre (II, 129), the storm caused 8000 deaths and 4 million pounds damage; 4000 trees were blown down in the New Forest.

[18] See Ken's letter to William Lloyd (the deprived Bishop of Norwich), 18 December 1703, quoted in Plumptre, II, 133: "I think I omitted to tell you the full of my deliverance in the late storm; for the house being searched the day following, the workmen found that the beam which supported the roof over my head was shaken out to that degree that it had but half an inch hold."

[19] See Lady Winchilsea, Introduction, pp. xxxvii–xl.

himself Bishop of Bath and Wells.[20] In the troubled year of 1685, Ken had held up Daniel as his ideal, "one that kept his station in the greatest revolutions that ever were."[21] He felt that this ideal should have been a practical possibility for a man of high principle as well as for the time-server. Unfortunately the church was not above politics, and change and uncertainty applied as much to the one as to the other. Ken was later to remark ruefully, "How oft the legislative power mistakes, / And prejudicial constitutions makes,"[22] and ironically admire the man "who takes in revolutions the right side."[23] In later years he became reconciled to a certain degree with the established church, and was critical of those non-jurors who placed sectarian interest above the welfare of the community.[24]

Ken never ceased however to castigate the timeservers against whom he had warned in his 1663 pamphlet. To Archbishop Tenison, whose funeral sermon on Queen Mary made no mention of her behaviour towards her father James II, he wrote with righteous indignation:

Did you know of no one injury or wrong she had done to any man, to whom she was to make amends to the uttermost of her power? Was the whole Revolution managed with that purity of intention, that perfect innocence, that exact justice, that tender charity, that irreproachable veracity, that there was nothing amiss in it? No remarkable failings, nothing that might deserve one penitent reflection? ... It is far from my intention here to dispute the lawfulness of the Revolution; yet I may say that I have never yet met any so bigoted to it, who would undertake to justify all the part which she as a daughter had in it... You complain, "Great is our loss of a most pious queen, in an atheistical and profane age... "But, sir, did not your heart smite you when you uttered this complaint? for I would fain know whether anything has more contributed to render the age atheistical and profane, ... than the prevarication of yourself and your time-serving brethren?[25]

[20] George Hooper (1640–1727) was at the Revolution one of the few decidedly high-churchmen to take the oaths, and he almost persuaded his friend Ken to do the same. *DNB*

[21] Ken, *Prose Works*, p. 89.

[22] "Edmund" VII, Ken, II, 196.

[23] "Hymnotheo," Ken, II, 58.

[24] See his letter to Lloyd (7 March 1704) where he complains of being pestered by the Bristol Jacobites. From 1704 Ken received from Queen Anne an annual pension of 200 pounds. Plumptre, II, 141, 150.

[25] *A Letter to Archbishop Tenison on his Funeral Sermon on Queen Mary* (1695), in Ken, *Prose Works*, pp. 303, 305. Ken had been chaplain to Mary before the Revolution. Thomas Tenison (1636–1715) became Archbishop of Canterbury in 1694 following the death of Tillotson. He further provoked Ken's displeasure by stretching his latitude to the point of preaching Nell Gwyn's funeral sermon. Out of favour in the last years of Queen Anne, he took active steps to secure the succession of George I. *DNB*

Such persuasive rancour from so gentle a man as Ken cannot have been stirred up without good cause. The religion of the Enlightenment would later provoke the equally saintly William Law to eloquent protest.

Ken was unwilling to equate those two pillars of Enlightenment religion, latitude and pietism. For the Cambridge Platonists latitude entailed pietism and vice versa; but in Ken's verse, written at a time when latitude had become the monopoly of an ecclesiastical and political establishment, pietism is associated with a virulent attack on latitude. The stage is thus set for a confrontation of opposites, which were to characterise the fortunes and failings of 18th century religion. At the turn of the century the split was beginning to be apparent.

Latitude meant the patriotic Protestant Anglican via media, broad enough based, thanks to occasional conformity, to build up a homogeneous social mood. Born of political compromise, it satisfied the majority. With Tillotson Archbishop of Canterbury, the consensus was broad enough to include all but the most stubborn of the Dissenters. Thus John Tutchin, of dissenting background, wrote a "Congratulary Poem to the Rev. Dr John Tillotson, Upon his Promotion to the Arch-Episcopal See of Canterbury" (1691), in which he described himself as one "who the Levite seldom did adore, / And scarce e'er knew a Priest I loved before."[26] And in America, Increase Mather claimed that, "had the sees in England fourscore years ago been filled with such Archbishops and Bishops as those which King William . . . has preferred to Episcopal dignity, there never had been a New England."[27] Tillotson himself portrayed the advantages of latitude based on a via media in these terms:

He that stands in the middle, is like to be more moderate towards the dissenters on both sides, than either of them will be to one another: because the middle is not so far from either extreme, as the extremes are from one another; at the worst, he stands fairest for an impartial inquiry after truth, and when he has satisfied himself where the truth lies, he may more silently pass over to it, without any great imputation of inconsistency; which cannot but be remarkable in him, who passeth from one extreme to another.[28]

[26] Quoted in Fairchild, I, 65. John Tutchin (1661–1707) was a Whig pamphleteer who took part in Monmouth's rebellion and was tried by Judge Jeffreys. In 1703 he came to the defence of Defoe with whom he collaborated on several projects. *DNB*

[27] "To the Reader," in Cotton Mather's *Johannes in Eremo* (1695). Quoted in L. G. Locke, p. 81. Increase Mather (1639–1723), distinguished New England Puritan and President of Harvard (1684–1701), was active in England from 1657–60 and from 1688–92. *DNB*

[28] Quoted in L. G. Locke, p. 68.

This argument is convincing. It is true that it is based on a smoothly concealed geometrical analogy rather than on reason, but it has all the bland force, all the sweet reasonableness, and none of the irony, of the art of Swiftian plausibility. What mattered to the archbishop was that it made good political sense.

Pietism on the other hand, however inevitably linked with latitude at its source, and in times of ecclesiastical tyranny often nourished by it, was beginning to spring its own roots in the consciences and sentiments of individual people. It was to become the specifically modern manifestation of the religious consciousness, and as such was retailed as early as 1705 by the journalist and Jack-of-all-trades, John Dunton:

> This plan to live by is entirely disencumbered of all those names, sects and parties that have raised so much dust and noise... The world it is true has given me that partial and precise name of Presbyterian; which I renounce for ever, and take opportunity to tell those strait-laced souls, who are for fixing bounds and enclosures in the flock of Christ, that I am neither Churchman, Independent, nor Quaker... I desire no character for the future but a lover of Jesus.[29]

Dunton's was the voice of the future; but Ken, though he deplored latitude, was not immune from the pietistic side of Enlightenment religion.

The brunt of Ken's attack on latitude can be found in the fifth book of "Edmund." Vertumno, who is described as having a "false Latitudinarian mind," presides over a devilish crew, who are the authors of every variety of ecclesiastical aberration, in a scene which was no doubt modelled on Milton's Hell. The catalogue of vices ascribed to the latitudinarian mind runs as follows: monstrous idols, pagan rites, impious prayers, schisms, heresies, vain philosophic schemes, rapts divine, perpetual doubt, new creeds, new modes of worship, and texts for every lie they utter. But above all, Vertumno's crew are accused of being "pliant to each revolution," and taking "the rising side" in church and state.[30] A few pages later, a devilish recipe of latitude, Erastianism and toleration is concocted for the consumption of Vertumno's followers:

> An Amplitude of Spirit you must have,
> Live to no words, to no religion slave.
> ....
> Religion and the evangelic law,

[29] Dunton, p. 20.
[30] Ken, II, 118–19.

Was only formed to keep the herd in awe.
. . . .
Tolerate all persuasions, cleave to none,
And Truth, whene'er 'tis hazardous, disown.[31]

A further glancing blow is cast in "Hymnotheo," where latitude is associated with the revival of old heresies,[32] and is satirised for disguising itself as the party of moderation.[33]

Latitude certainly led to deism, amongst other things; and this old heresy Ken chooses to satirise and pity, rather than controvert by argument. The pity is to be found in the lyrical "Anodynes," where he complains:

The Deists, God in show confess,
Yet want supports in their distress;
Their God has ne'er revealed his will,
No promise made to help in ill.[34]

And the satire occurs in this passage from "Hymnotheo":

The Deists, who of Atheism grow ashamed,
To suit their vices, a fit Numen framed;
One who exacts no worship, gives no laws,
Who sinners with no fear of judgment awes;
Who while he snores in intermundian ease,
Precarious votaries act whate'er they please:
Thus by the God they for themselves have made,
They Deity, not honour, but degrade;
This modern idol hellish Fraud contrived,
Deism is sinking Paganism revived.[35]

Ken's attack on latitude is thus very much an attack on the deistic tendencies of latitude, and is delivered from a position of religious experience rather than ecclesiastical party.

Pietism is to the religious mind what scepticism is to the secular. There is the same refusal to engage in epistemological argument, the same suspicion that philosophical or theological concepts are meaningless. On the rare occasions when Ken takes up a philosophical position, it is in an attempt to reinforce the validity of religious experience. Unlike Henry More, who sought unceasingly to give philosophical explanations and justifications for his religious position, Ken can in no way be said to have embraced Cartesianism, or any other

[31] Ken, II, 121.
[32] Ken, III, 223.
[33] Ken, III, 224.
[34] Ken, III, 426.
[35] Ken, III, 296–7.

system. He rarely strikes even the faintest Cartesian note. In the introduction to his poems, he notes that Philhymno, his muse, has swept clean from "rubbish notions" the cells of his memory, and stored in them "all the clear ideas."[36] And in one of this more intellectual lyrics, he uses the Cartesian *Cogito, ergo sum*, "Thought life infers," to illustrate his argument that mutability applies to the mind as well as the body.[37] But elsewhere he draws on Descartes only indirectly, to write lyrics about infinity. Like many a post-Cartesian poet, he is obsessed with obtaining "some clear idea ... of Infinite."[38] Similarly Ken shows little interest in Newtonian and Royal Society theory about the universe, beyond noting in a long Pindaric, entitled "Providence," that.

> Should God sit idle, and his Influence stop,
> Into a wild disorder all would drop.[39]

and being pleased

> To see all Nature's course,
> Harmonious kept by gravitating force.[40]

If Ken had had Henry More's intellectual curiosity and taste for philosophical system, there can be little doubt that he would have argued in favour of the extension of the spiritual universe. Pepys recalls two lively discussions he had with Ken about the existence of spirits, but Ken does not pursue in his verse a matter which Pepys's scepticism had led him to treat in conversation.[41] Only in one passage of "Hymnotheo" does Ken argue against materialism. He takes the Platonic view that matter is visible only because it is dressed; spirit and undressed matter are equally beyond sense-perception:

> Some immaterial being would disclaim,
> Since they of that could no idea frame;

[36] Ken, I, 12.
[37] "Life," Ken, IV, 40.
[38] "Infinity," in "Hymns on the Attributes of God" (separate pagination), Ken, II, 6.
[39] "Hymns," Ken, II, 122.
[40] "Hymns," Ken, II, 145.
[41] See Samuel Pepys, *Diary*, 2 September 1683: "At supper ... discourse about Spirits. Dr Ken asserting there were such, and I with the rest, denying it." 11 September 1683: "After supper ... Dr Ken and I very hot in dispute about Spirits." Quoted in Rice, p. 58. Pepys and Ken were on a government expedition to Tangier. Pepys appreciated Ken's pulpit eloquence, but could not stomach his unscientific approach: "Dr Ken made an excellent sermon, full of the skill of a preacher, but nothing of a natural philosopher, it being all forced meat." *Diary*, 23 September 1683, quoted in Plumptre, I, 167.

They might as well material things deny,
Since matter ne'er was naked to the eye.[42]

A few pages later he comes up with the occasionalist argument as put forward by Malebranche and modified by Berkeley. Addressing his soul, he writes:

My bulk is sepulchre, is only shell,
And what within inhabits, cannot tell;
'Tis by thy rays all other things I see.[43]

But far from relying on such scraps of philosophy, Ken insists that spiritual reality and the spiritual life must be based on experience.

Ken is for ever saying that grace is a matter of experience, not of thought:

How thou, who wilt not heaven forsake,
Canst in my heart thy mansion make,
Is by Experience taught,
Though it transcends my thought.[44]

In his *Exposition of the Church Catechism* for the people of his diocese, the emphasis is the same: "The love of God is a grace rather to be felt than defined."[45] Confronted with the mystery of the Trinity, he exclaims: "Though I cannot conceive thee, yet let me daily experiment thy goodness."[46] In the lyrics his pietism runs rampant in an attempt to escape the bonds of epistemology:

Let Learning vain employ its hours,
To state God's Grace in all its powers;
In my own heart enflamed, may I
Its operations dear descry;
Experience in one minute more will teach,
Than Speculation in an age can reach.[47]

Most of the lyrics are in fact descriptions of these operations, or, when grace fails, attempts to rouse the flagging spirit with "inflammatives more tender."[48] Ken is thus more interested in God the Saviour, than

[42] Ken, III, 294.
[43] Ken, III, 298.
[44] "Jesus Present," Ken, I, 425.
[45] Ken, *Prose Works*, p. 118.
[46] *Ibid.*, p. 126.
[47] "God's Grace," in "Hymns," Ken, II, 108–9. The tone and message of the final couplet is similar to that of Wordsworth's "The Tables Turned": "One impulse from a vernal wood/May teach you more of man,/Of moral evil and of good,/Than all the sages can." Wordsworth, *The Poetical Works*, ed. T. Hutchinson, revised Ernest de Selincourt (London: Oxford University Press, 1936), p. 377.
[48] "Christophil," Ken, I, 419.

in God the Creator – "'twas much greater Love mankind to save, / Than that which being gave."[49]

The theology of pietism has its own vocabulary. Underlying this vocabulary is the basic refusal to investigate or define modes, an unwillingness to know, for example, "How Thou from nothing didst the world create," on the grounds that

> Nor mystery, nor scientific scheme,
> Nor miracle is now, dear Lord, thy theme;
> Humility is all thou wouldst impart.[50]

Law and Byrom would make even more of this theology, rejecting the slavery of cause and effect, and resolving spiritual learning into knowledge of the will of God. Ken follows this Augustinian emphasis when he writes:

> Why should the Schools employ their stress,
> In studying only how to guess;
> We the true Cause assign,
> In naming Will Divine;
> While learned Ignorance in vain shall strive,
> Into the Manner, how God works, to dive.[51]

Such theology was not new; nor was it peculiar to an age of Enlightenment. Even in the middle ages, men had sought to escape the bondage of mechanical literalism, which a theology expressed in terms of Aristotelian cause and effect inevitably entailed. In the 11th century Durandus of Troarn had reduced all controversy over the eucharist to the incontrovertible pietistic formula, "Motum sentimus: modum nescimus: praesentiam credimus."[52] And at the beginning of the 17th century, Lancelot Andrewes, with whose works Ken must have been familiar, employed the same formula in his controversy with Cardinal Bellarmine: "We believe no less than you that the presence is real. Concerning the method of the presence, we define nothing rashly."[53]

In the course of the 17th century, such intellectual prudence came

[49] *Ibid.*
[50] "The Humility of Jesus," Ken, I, 459.
[51] "God's Will," in "Hymns," Ken, II, 73.
[52] This slogan was quoted by John Bramhall in his *Answer to M. de la Milletière* (1653), and is attributed to Durandus of Troarn (c. 1020–88), a Benedictine monk whose *Liber de Corpore et Sanguine Christi Contra Berengarium et Eius Sectatores* appeared c. 1060. See P. E. More and F. L. Cross (ed.), *Anglicanism* (London: Society for the Propagation of Christian Knowledge, 1935), p. 484.
[53] Lancelot Andrewes, *Responsio ad Apologiam Cardinalis Bellarmini* (1610). Quoted in More and Cross, p. 464.

to be the norm in all fields of learning, but especially in the realm of metaphysical speculation. Locke laid the foundations for the philosophy of the English Enlightenment by subjecting metaphysics to the insights of pietism:

I content myself with ignorance, which roundly thinks thus: God is a simple being, omniscient, that knows all things possible; and omnipotent, that can do or make all things possible. But how he knows, or how he makes, I do not conceive: his ways of knowing as well as his ways of creating are to me incomprehensible; if they were not so, I should not think him to be God.[54]

Not even a preromantic enthusiast could overcome the intellectual prudence endemic to the 18th century. In the words of Henry Brooke:

Whate'er the spark, the light, the lamp, the ray,
Essence, or effluence of essential day,
Substance or transubstantiate, and enshrined,
Soul, spirit, reason, intellect or mind;
Or these but terms, that dignify the use
Of some unknown, some entity abstruse –
Perception specifies the sacred guest,
Appropriate to the individual breast.[55]

By refusing to define modes, Ken was participating in a movement which had far-reaching effects on the nature and scope of thought; for pietism in the 18th century affected not only theology, but also philosophy and science, politics and government.

On more than one occasion Ken seeks to support and clarify his theological vocabulary with an analogy from the nature of man, and in particular the nature of vision or perception. As he says,

I objects see; yet in my brain,
How Vision's made, cannot explain;
My Soul the Spirit working feels,
While modes of working he conceals;
When God makes in our souls abode,
'Tis curiosity, to search the mode.[56]

Berkeley was to use a similar argument:

To me it seems evident that if none but those who had nicely examined, and could themselves explain, the principle of individuation in man, or

54 John Locke, "An Examination of Malebranche," in *Works* (9 vols.; 12th ed.; London: Rivington, 1824), VIII, 255.

55 Henry Brooke, *Universal Beauty*, IV, 7–14, in Alexander Chalmers (ed.), *The Works of the English Poets from Chaucer to Cowper* (21 vols.; London: J. Johnson, 1810), XVII, 351.

56 "Jesus Love Preserved," Ken, I, 501.

untie the knots and answer the objections which may be raised even about human personal identity, would require of us to explain the divine mysteries, we should not be often called upon for a clear and distinct idea of *person* in relations to the Trinity, nor would the difficulties on that head be often objected to our faith.[57]

Berkeley's solution to these difficulties of course went beyond a pietistic fideism; he sought to reconcile science and religion with his carefully argued philosophical concept of "optic language."[58] But Ken's diagnosis of the problem already resembles Berkeley's as much as it resembles Lancelot Andrewes', and all three derive their arguments from the central Anglican tradition of a via media. For Ken and Berkeley, the via media lies between Malebranchian occasionalism and Hobbesian materialism.

In the didactic lyric "Omniscience," Ken develops the analogy with vision further:

Of objects we ideas frame,
But how into our heads they came;
From whence their being springs,
And likeness to known things;
How in our intellectual hive,
Mind their distinct apartments can contrive;

No human intellect can solve.
Yet when Omniscience we revolve;
Audacious men will try,
To grasp Infinity;
They might more easily contain
In cockle-shell the whole Atlantic Main.

From our internal pictures, we
Ideas feign in Deity;
And our Creator tie,
Those images to eye;
Thus God, while the universe he made,
We to a mean artificer degrade.[59]

Ken does not often argue, but he was clearly persuaded that this analogy was useful as a support for the validity of religious experience.

57 Berkeley, p. 298 (Euphranor is speaking).

58 In *Alciphron* Berkeley briefly sums up the religious implications of his theory of vision. Crito dismisses the occasionalist hypothesis: "As for that metaphysical hypothesis, I can make no more of it than you. But I think it plain this optic language hath a necessary connexion with knowledge, wisdom and goodness. It is equivalent to a constant creation, betokening an immediate act of power and providence. It cannot be accounted for by mechanical principles, by atoms, attractions or effluvia." *Ibid.*, p. 159.

59 "Omniscience," in "Hymns," Ken, II, 70–1.

A passage in "Hymnotheo" takes up the theme, extending the analogy to light, sound, geometry and gravity, but arriving at a conclusion identical to that of "Omniscience":

> Men, who to search the eye or ear intent,
> In that sole study a long life have spent,
> At last acknowledge ignorance profound
> Of the true nature of or light or sound;
> All in extension of a line agree;
> Yet none know how its parts connected be;
> All men in bodies gravity confess,
> Yet its true nature none could ever guess;
> Proud Atheists then their ignorance should own,
> Who cannot solve the falling of a stone.
> Vain men bind God to low mechanic rules,
> To the absurd conjectures of the Schools.[60]

The pietism expressed in Ken's verse is not sectarian. He may have written from a position of excluded high-churchmanship, but what he wrote reflects the atmosphere of his age, and provides an interesting link between the Caroline and Augustan phases of the English religious consciousness.

[60] Ken, III, 313.

CHAPTER THREE

THE AESTHETICS OF INFINITY

Before we measure the strength of the Metaphysical tradition in Ken's verse, we should show the disintegration of this tradition in the wake of two kinds of Enlightenment aesthetic, the aesthetics of infinity and neoclassicism. Both were suited to the purposes and mood of pietism, the one allowing a crude expressionism with scope for unconfined sublimity, the other offering a strictly regulated Parnassian alternative for moments when enthusiasm flagged and it became necessary, with the steadying help of poetic diction, to point to what was obvious, agreed and social in religious experience.

Ken's attitude towards poetry, like Plato's, is ambiguous. On the one hand he shares the Cambridge Platonists' distrust of the imagination:

> Whether I will or no,
> Imagination out will go,
> In its licentious flights,
> It disagreeing forms unites,
> Forms monstruous, Atheistic, or unclean,
> And strives with darling vice my conscience to serene.
> Sin the internal cells
> Invades, where my remembrance dwells;
> Past foul ideas there,
> In lively colours pictured are;
> When to recall truths heavenly I designed,
> Things sensual overspread the surface of my mind.[1]

And on the other hand he maintains that the poet is concerned with divine matter:

> No Atheists Brutes to Poets could refine,
> All own that Grace for Matter too divine.[2]

1 "Psyche," Ken, IV, 200.
2 "Hymnotheo," Ken, III, 300.

This is an ambiguity which is resolved in the aesthetics of neoclassical pietism as formulated by Norris, Watts, Dennis, Blackmore, Thomson, and a host of other poets and literary theorists of the Enlightenment. With the rise of science, the threat posed by the imagination disappeared. By the beginning of the 18th century the imagination was associated with a barbaric and unscientific past and there was reckoned to be no danger in either the embroidery of fancy or indulgence in the sublime.

This ambiguity is not the only manifestation of Ken's relevance to aesthetics. In his rambling, formless epic, "Urania or the Spouse's Garden," he describes the failure of what can only be called Renaissance aesthetics to support his poetic inspiration. The passage is itself rhetorical, an attempt to declare the ineffable by discovering that no rule of rhetoric can do his love justice; and yet the complaint seems to articulate in a particularly telling way what so much of Ken's verse suggests, namely the inability of rhetoric, as practised by Renaissance poets, to do justice to the plainer and more obvious emotions expressed by the late 17th century:

> No metaphors her loveliness can paint,
> Or how I love the Saint.
>
> On flowers, gems, sun, moon, stars, I gaze,
> From them expressions strive to raise,
> But find no heights of speech
> Her excellence can reach,
> And no poetic rapture can declare
> The love to her I bear.[3]

We have to wait over twenty pages for the rhetorical and vaguely Metaphysical application of this passage to the purpose of amorous persuasion:

> O stay with me till in my heart, fair Saint,
> I your Idea paint.[4]

Ken had not abandoned the practice of raising expressions and finding heights of speech, but he was moving forward to an aesthetics of pietism similar to that held by Norris, Dennis and Watts.

"Urania" meanders on for another thirty pages before we come across a description of Ken's poetic ideal:

[3] "Urania," Ken, IV, 423.
[4] *Ibid.*, IV, 449.

A poet should have heat and light,
Of all things a capacious sight,
Serenity with rapture joined,
Aims noble, eloquence refined,
Strong, modest, sweetness to endear,
Expressions lively, lofty, clear.

High thoughts, an admirable theme,
For decency a chaste esteem,
Of harmony a perfect skill,
Just characters of good and ill,
And all concentred souls to please,
Instruct, inflame, melt, calm, and ease.

Such graces can nowhere be found,
Unless on consecrated ground,
Where poets fix on God their thought,
By sacred inspiration taught.[5]

The poetic qualities in demand are those of the 18th century. "Capacious sight" and "lofty expressions" characterise the Pindaric, the prospect poem, the sublime, and the natural description of Enlightenment poetry. "Serenity," "clear expression" and refined "eloquence" characterise the poetic diction of neoclassicism. We shall see how Ken sought to practise what he preached.

Ken goes further than his predecessors, though not as far as Edward Young, in lyricising space and infinity. In many of his lyrics space takes over from God as the object of devotion; it becomes the poet's natural habitat. Ken's space is rather less physical than that of the Newtonian enthusiasts; it has just enough presence to provide a short cut to God via the attribute of infinity, but no more. Space is used to provide religious illumination and make spiritual discoveries. In "Christophil" Ken's soul has to

Fly over all imaginable Space,
Outgoings of Love Infinite to trace;
While thou in Aether hovering art above.
Discover all the unknown lands of Love.[6]

Space thus becomes a substitute for imagination as well as for God. Movement and objects, which in the human imagination would give rise to licentious flights, disagreeing forms and sensual pictures, are somehow whitewashed and acceptable in the new-found virgin lands of space. There is just enough movement – "fly," "outgoings,"

[5] *Ibid.*, IV, 477.
[6] Ken, I, 417.

"trace," "hovering," "discover" – and just enough physical presence – "Love," "Aether," "lands" – to give poetic substance to the muse's flight. Too often however the flight is an escape from both humanity and poetry.

In "Infinity" Ken acknowledges the nature of an obsession which colours so much of his rhapsodic lyricism. As he says,

> I oft have sent abroad my Mind,
> With a commission unconfined;
> Some clear Idea in its flight,
> To bring me back of Infinite.[7]

Space is thus principally a means of exploring one attribute of the Godhead; but there are also signs of a more mundane purpose, namely the celebration of God's providence in the world of nature and men. In the poem entitled "Providence," Ken begins conventionally enough:

> My swiftest envoy, Thought, fly out,
> Range all about;
> O'er the celestial circle fly,
> God's providential footsteps to descry.[8]

The introspective imperative, and the vaguely Metaphysical conjunction of the remote "celestial circle" and the familiar "footsteps," point to a poet who has not yet purged his style according to Enlightenment criteria. But in the course of the poem, which runs to over thirty pages, it becomes obvious that the 18th century is not far away. There are hints of the physico-theological versifier:

> Thought first a voyage took,
> The vegetable realm to overlook.[9]

There is the note of the Newtonian enthusiast, celebrating

> Nature's course,
> Harmonious kept by gravitating force.[10]

And there is even a hint of the Thomsonian commercial theme, with Thought seeing "stately ships ... through the world spread intercourse of gain."[11] We should expect this from a Whig as early as the

[7] Ken, II, 6.
[8] Ken, II, 113.
[9] Ken, II, 114.
[10] Ken, II, 145.

1690s, but it blends as badly with Ken's usual tone and subject-matter as with his politics.

Ken exploited the possibilities of space not only to sing the mind's flight to its maker, but also to indulge in that favourite Enlightenment pastime, the prospect. The prospect could be used to stamp the religious lyric with the mark of pietism. The lyricist is not so much concerned with justifying himself or representing his own spiritual struggles and triumphs, as drawing, often in pictorial and always in static form, the convincing evidence of faith. This evidence was thought to be obvious to all; it had but to be pointed at, and enlightened, to command the assent of all reasonable creatures. Space is thus used as a theatre in which to display the glorious evidences of the Christian religion, and the poet's flight and aspiration is rewarded with a comprehensive and convincing view. Ken's prospects differ from those of the 18th century only in that their space is occasionally peopled with intelligences, faded relics of Dantesque visions. Thus in the same poem that briefly celebrates Britain's mercantile spirit,

> Thought, who on swifter wing can mount on high,
> And in one pulse, the stars' whole circle fly;
> To gain a Prospect clear,
> Flew to the Intelligence, who tends the upper sphere.[12]

But Ken's prospects are usually empty; they merely indicate that one has arrived. Love is the commonest terminus. But the view is so distant that no details are filled in. Ken may say, "Oft has my mind took flight, / For Prospects of Love infinite,"[13] but his love is eaten up by his infinity, and our view is vague.

"Christophil" offers prospects in two directions, of heaven above, and earth below. On the one hand "Mind" had "all the world in intellectual view";[14] on the other hand, "of the heavenly sphere, / And Jesus' glories, he had prospect clear."[15] Elsewhere we are told that "Love from intellectual sight, / Takes its first rise and gains its height";[16] and the poet promises, "I'll clear your intellectual view / Of things, to form Ideas true."[17] But nowhere does Ken fill in the

[11] Ken, II, 115.
[12] Ken, II, 138.
[13] "Unity," Ken II 36.
[14] Ken I, 418.
[15] Ken, I, 421.
[16] "God Known Through Jesus," Ken, I, 465.
[17] "Hymnotheo," Ken, III, 265.

prospect he has cleared. It is always an end in itself, yet vague and without sinews. The 18th century would produce a proliferation of prospects, views of both nature and grace, in which careful choice of detail implied totality and offered convincing evidence of God's providence. Ken's prospects are colourless because they are not yet detached from the eye of the beholder. In a sense Ken was right when he said that his poems "loftiest prospects have disclosed, / On brinks of bright eternity composed."[18] But to the reader it is obvious that such prospects and such brinks are not primarily spatial ones, however much Ken's taste for the aesthetics of infinity might suggest the contrary. Such brinks and prospects as do occur are Metaphysical. Far from constituting a public display of evidences in the 18th century sense, they reveal an intensity and openness of lyric thought, and provide a record of spiritual ups and downs.

It is thus misleading to place Ken in the tradition of pietist aesthetics as apotheosised in Young, without remarking that all Ken's best instincts, and any poetic achievement we wish to credit him with go against the grain of this trend towards the Enlightenment. Ken's pietism led him to condemn the inductive methods of science, and far from wanting the logic of love to follow the same path, from finite to infinite, from the familiar to the sublime, he claimed that love's method was exactly opposite to that of science:

All Sciences one method keep,
From shallow truths to wade too deep;
In Love the method is reversed,
That first is in abstruse immersed;
From what it never comprehends,
It to familiar truths descends.[19]

This method followed by love is the method of the 17th century mind. Norris believed in this method, and built up a philosophy from it. Fénelon, following Malebranche, asserted: "C'est dans l'infini que je vois le fini."[20]

The English Enlightenment on the other hand rejected such rhapsodic doggerel. Watts, who admired Fénelon, would have nothing to do with him when he followed Malebranche, and picked on this particular point as "very weakly written ... and built upon an enthusiastical and mistaken scheme."[21] Locke's comment on Fénelon's

[18] Ken, I, Dedication.
[19] "Philanthropy," Ken, I, 508–9.
[20] Fénelon, *De l'existence et des attributs de Dieu* (Paris: Didot, 1853), p. 143.
[21] *The Improvement of the Mind*, Watts, V, 218.

view is strikingly characteristic:

We are told that we have not only the idea of infinite, but before that of finite. This being a thing of experience, everyone must examine himself; . . . it being my misfortune to find it otherwise in myself.[22]

Watts and Locke did not believe in starting from the abstruse; for them a descent from the abstruse to the familiar, from the infinite to the finite, could have no meaning.

Ken's verse, to the extent that it lies in the Metaphysical tradition, cultivates this descent. In this respect it belongs to the literature of sacramental piety rather than aspiring pietism. But Ken is not immune to the flights of aspiration, and in the same poem that he defines the logic of love as descent from infinite to finite, he rhapsodises on the theme of reciprocal love in the language of Leibnizian complacency:

From thy love, mine, begins its flights,
My love, fresh love, in thee excites,
Thou lovest, and I love again,
Reciprocations we'll maintain,
Till centring Lord in thee above,
I can have no increase of love.[23]

Ken seems unaware of any inconsistency, and is prepared to condemn in another context the aspiring mind he here celebrates. In "Hymnotheo" he writes:

Philosophers o'er the globe terraqueous roam,
To find that bliss they might possess at home;
Strange madness on the sea and in the dark,
To seek that shore at which they all embark.[24]

When the philosophers aspire, they are on the sea and in the dark; when Ken himself aspires, he maintains reciprocations with his God. Ken reminds us that, if in the 1690s the aesthetics of infinity were a fashionable force to be reckoned with, they were not the only option available to the religious lyricist.

[22] Locke, "An Examination of Malebranche," *Works*, VIII, 231.
[23] "Philanthropy," Ken, I, 510.
[24] Ken, III, 241.

CHAPTER FOUR

NEOCLASSICISM

Ken may have had little success as an exponent of the aesthetics of infinity, but he certainly had a minor talent as a neoclassicist. He was too much of a Metaphysical poet to make any sense of the vast tracts of space newly open to the poets of the Enlightenment; but he was not too much of a Metaphysical to feel at home in the secure confines of the couplet. It was of course a safer medium than the Pindaric for the minor poet; it favoured the mediocre without encouraging the downright bad. And yet it is unusual to find a devotional poet taking so readily to a medium tailored primarily to the needs of the worldly satirist.

The Restoration had expressed itself in the couplet over a whole generation, so much so that Prior, writing in 1689 before Ken had turned to verse, condemned in one breath the materialism of the mechanistic philosophy and the Parnassian jingle of the juggling rhymesters; these "crabbed rogues, that read Lucretius," maintain

> That writing is but just like dice;
> And lucky mains make people wise:
> That jumbled words, if Fortune throw 'em,
> Shall, well as Dryden, form a poem;
> . . . .
> So atoms dancing round the centre,
> They urge, made all things at a venture.[1]

Prior's view is important, for he was a sceptic and something of a pietist, whose suspicions of Enlightenment claims, wittily set down in his *Alma*, offered alternative reading, in the genre of philosophic epic, to those 18th century minds which, like John Wesley's, could not

[1] Matthew Prior, "Epistle to Fleetwood Shepherd" (1689), lines 57, 71–4, 77–8, *The Literary Works*, ed. H. B. Wright and M. K. Spears (2 vols.; Oxford: Clarendon Press, 1959), I, 87.

stomach the deistic bias of Pope's *Essay on Man.* Ken was more to Wesley's taste than even Prior; but although writing at the same time as Prior, he belonged to a previous generation, and had less scruples about using the idiom of the court, at which he had been a distinguished if somewhat incongruous personality.

What is even more incongruous than Ken's celebrated encounters with Nell Gwyn is his taste for the spirit as well as the techniques of the couplet. His epics roll on in splendid mediocrity and rarely rise to the level of art; their remote metaphysical subject-matter, and their reliance on outlandish spiritual machinery, only alienate the reader's sympathies. And yet, every now and then, comes a passage which deserves notice by virtue of strength of syntax, satiric energy, or mastery of antithesis. Such passages suggest that Marvell is not the only point of contact between the particular strength of Metaphysical poetry and the full-blooded classicism of the great Tory satirists. Only, while in Marvell the two elements blend, in Ken, even more than in Cowley, they are totally separate. While the affinities between Marvell and Swift illuminate the development from Metaphysical to Augustan, Ken's affinities with, say Herbert and Crashaw on the one hand, and Dryden and Pope on the other, merely spotlight the disparate characteristics of two distinct ages.

"Edmund" and "Hymnotheo" are written almost exclusively according to neoclassical aesthetics. If Ken was a Metaphysical poet by instinct, he was an Augustan by artistry. He knows for example how to make witty profit out of the pathetic fallacy, as in this passage from the early pages of "Edmund":

> The morning stars had sang their early lay,
> And with their music waked the sluggish day;
> Who with half-open eyelids straight disclosed
> A rosy blush that he so long reposed.[2]

Such wit is not a gratuitous light-hearted flourish on Ken's part; he believed – and religious men continued to do so well into the 18th century – that it was sinful to get up late. The stylistic trick is thus heavily conscious and knowing in the way 18th century poetry set out to be. On the whole however Ken's couplets are striking when they are straightforwardly and outspokenly polemical or satirical. In such passages it is possible to distinguish between a primitive, and usually alliterative, force of language, and a more advanced and subtle strength of syntax based on antithesis.

[2] Ken, II, 20.

One of the reasons for Ken's relative success as a neoclassical practitioner is his ability to adapt the language and tone of Biblical and preaching invective to the limited scope of the couplet. Well over half the passages inviting comparison with Dryden and Pope have as their subject-matter one of the seven deadly sins, usually lust. And when lust raises its ugly head, alliteration abounds to chop it off. Ken's taste for alliterative violence may offend the canons of Augustan politeness, and lead him to indulge in material too crude for the subtle refinement the couplet demands; but it also shows that Dryden and Pope owed much to a native tradition older than the couplet and with its roots in the language of Langland and the popular sermon. Ken conserves the energy of this tradition, and yet manages to prune it to the stab and run tactics of pointed antithesis:

Those lustful fools and those lewd filthy queans,
Antedate in their bones infernal pains;
Endure a lingering martyrdom for lust,
And live corruption ere they turn to dust.

Lust is followed by Gluttony:

Those fools their appetites with dainties glut,
They make a God of their voracious gut;
Strive their foul curiosities to please,
And fuel heap for Lust and for Disease.[3]

The alliteration is alleviated by the satiric wit of the antithetical "live corruption" / "turn to dust" and "God" / "gut." Apart from the first line in which the subject-matter is established, there is no overloading of epithets; and apart from the message of the second line, nothing extraneous to the logic and rhythm of the couplet's economy.

In an epic the couplet cannot always be the vehicle of satiric wit. Description and action must have their place. In such passages, which form the bulk of the narrative, Ken rarely rises above the downright mediocre. He is however capable of a Homeric or Miltonic simile which is fitting as well as picturesque:

As a tall stag whose lustful force is spent,
To damp the offensive rankness of his scent,
In shades remote to dig his mould retires,
And rolling in new earth, his stink perspires:

[3] Ken, II, 82–3.

Thus Satan to the sweet Arabia flew,
And on the spicy beds his carcass threw;
On odorous plants he rolled it to and fro,
To suck the effluviums which he smelt out-flow.[4]

And there are times when the alliteration is entirely appropriate to the action:

By her inveigling locks he seized the whore,
Her own foul philtre down her throat to pour;
To fetch full force, her carcass round he swung,
And into neighbouring Hell the strumpet flung.[5]

Unfortunately such deeds of heroism are few and far between. But that they exist at all is worthy of notice in an early Augustan who is not translating Homer. What the Augustans gained in politeness they lost in energy. Only Pope, whose Homer was hailed as the masterpiece of the age, combined a maximum of both. Ken's technique indicates that there was a living tradition on which Pope could draw to create his masterpiece.

Ken's own reliance on tradition is obvious. Pope would not have been ashamed of "For lust or lucre she no man refused,"[6] nor would the Restoration wits have scorned Ken's picture of the young hero about town:

Lewd company there Vice familiarise,
By impious talk his spirit atheise:
He of a Beau much courted the esteem,
And thought it wit and breeding to blaspheme;
Foul, leprous Queans, as Basilisks, by view,
Their poisonous breath out in their kisses threw.[7]

But too often Ken's saintly obsession with the sins of lust leads to over-writing. What would Addison have thought of this strange medieval survival?

I fell soon as to rise I did begin,
Alternating repentances and sin:
As clean-washed swine return into their sty,
And in their stinking mire re-wallowing lie;
As dogs, the filthy vomits they cast up,
In a short space with appetite re-sup:

[4] Ken, II, 91.
[5] Ken, II, 113.
[6] Ken, II, 261.
[7] "Hymnotheo," Ken, III, 63–4.

Thus to all sins which I abjured I flew,
A filthier ordure, a more loathsome spew.[8]

The repetitive adjectives and the outlandish "re-wallowing" drown the similes in a welter of abuse. The same pedestrian insistence, regardless of poetic effect, colours Ken's attempts at Spenserian allegory:

Moria on a gaudy throne sits down,
Upon her head she wears a glittering crown;
With her false gems she makes a dazzling glare,
Thick dawbed with paint, to make her seeming fair;
Perfumed with odorous quintessence, and dressed
In a loose trailing rainbow-coloured vest.[9]

The structure of each couplet is thrown away, and the verse evaporates into bathos. On other occasions, by contrast, Ken winds his couplets too tight, and the weight of antithesis smothers the meaning. Thus:

Her mind instable, her devotion dead,
Care seized her heart, and impious thoughts her head.[10]

Hope absence, faith obscurity implies,
Charity only to fruition flies.[11]

In darkness martyrs, angels dwell in light;
Yet martyrs' faith may vie with angels' sight.[12]

The artistry of these couplets saves them from bathos, but is subservient to, rather than coextensive with, the doctrinal message.

Ken often makes competent use of antithesis. On such occasions he manipulates the couplet with skill, avoiding the pitfalls of overwriting, bathos and preciosity. Even his bête noire, the Great Whore, comes across forcefully in the controlled grotesquerie of the following:

See how she sits perfumed, thick painted, curled,
The lewd, the common strumpet of the world;
On her cursed bulk she wears a scarlet robe,
Rolling her eyes and venom o'er the globe;
In precious gems, and orient pearls arrayed,
Which by the stench she breathes in lustre fade.[13]

[8] *Ibid.*, III, 119.
[9] *Ibid.*, III, 191.
[10] "Psyche," Ken, IV, 262.
[11] "Hymnotheo," Ken, III, 165.
[12] "Edmund," Ken, II, 348.
[13] "Hymnotheo," Ken, III, 271.

The third line is almost a weak link, but the energy of "bulk" and the functional simplicity of the syntax saves it from bathos. Otherwise the Spenserian subject-matter is nicely tailored to the economy of the couplet, thanks in part to the antithetical "eyes" / "venom" and "stench" / "lustre." Alliteration has almost disappeared, and indeed there is less of it in "Hymnotheo" than there is in "Edmund." There is no evidence that "Hymnotheo" is later than "Edmund," but it is marked by a more competent use of alliteration, which is saved to wind up a paragraph rather than drawn on to cloy each and every couplet:

> When they have watched and sweat and toiled,
> The world and their own souls embroiled,
> And by a thousand acts unjust,
> Have tried to sate their sensual lust,
> They feel the bubble which they gain
> Is volatile, vexatious, vain.[14]

This is an advanced way of using alliteration, clinching an argument by moving from the physical ("volatile"), through the psychological ("vexatious"), to the moral ("vain").[15] Ken can also make the couplet shine on its own, curled round its nuclear antithesis:

> Sage Epicurus best could Gods devise,
> Gods for the mob, but idle for the wise.[16]

But he is at his best working within the unit of the paragraph, when a spurt of witty antitheses is underlined in the concluding drawnout chord.

A good example of paragraphic organisation is to be found in his description of Sloth:

> Cast your eye down on that dull slothful wight,
> He no distinctions knows 'twixt day and night;

[14] *Ibid.*, III, 183.

[15] Cf. Pope's couplet:

> "She glares in *Balls*, *Front-boxes*, and the *Ring*,
> A vain, unquiet, glitt'ring, wretched Thing!"

"Epistle to Miss Blount, With the Works of Voiture" (1710), in Alexander Pope, *Poems*, ed. J. Butt (London: Methuen, 1963), p. 170. Here Pope reproduces Ken's subtlety, moving from the moral ("vain"), through the psychological ("unquiet"), to the physical ("glitt'ring").

[16] "Hymnotheo," Ken, III, 222. Ken possibly had Dryden's couplet in mind:

> "Gods they had tri'd of every shape and size.
> That God-smiths could produce or Priests devise."

Absalom and Achitophel (1681), I, 49–50, in John Dryden, *Poems*, ed. J. Sargeaunt (London: Oxford University Press, 1910), p. 50. Cf. also a more specific parallel to Ken's point in *The Medall* (1682), lines 276–84, in *ibid.*, p. 87.

Care and fixed thought are torments to his mind,
He lives a very cypher of mankind;
When he is waked, he for more sleep will cry,
And all the time he lives, he strives to die;
Conjures the world to let him snort alone,
An useless, lazy, intermundian drone.[17]

And the longer paragraph on the latitudinarians is by far the best sustained piece of couplet-writing in Ken's verse. It is sustained for two reasons. Firstly it categorises human follies in Hudibrastic style and with an energy worthy of Dryden; and secondly the competence of the antithetical techniques is reinforced by Ken's personal involvement in the subject-matter:

O'er them they chose Vertumno to preside;
In whose false Latitudinarian mind
All the delusions scattered there combined;
There they at several forges Errors frame,
And each assumes Truth's venerable name:
One monstrous idols forms, and pagan rites;
Another charms that impious prayers indites:
Here they raise schisms, there heresies compound,
There disputatious wranglers Truth confound;
Here they design vain philosophic schemes,
And make the gospel prostrate to their dreams;
There half-learned clubs fallacious volumes vend;
Here critics spoil the authors they amend;
There proud enthusiasts boast of rapts divine;
There sceptics to perpetual doubt incline;
There they for wavering minds new creeds collect,
These by new modes of worship glean a sect;
Those scripture read, delusion to promote,
And texts for every lie they utter, quote;
False prophets here false pleasing things presage,
And wrest the Apocalypse to fool the age;
Others new saints by false ideas draw,
And credulous souls by lying wonders awe;
That flying squadron to no sect adheres,
But pliant to each revolution veers,
They are around by giddy spirits whirled,
Antarctic to the crown, but towards the world;
Soon as they waking see the dawning ray,
They ask, What wind of doctrine blows today?
Their consciences with interest transact,
All things or nothing they believe or act;

[17] "Edmund," Ken, II, 83–4.

The rising side in Church, in State they take,
Which when it sinks, the vermin all forsake.[18]

Such comptence is neither "pedestrian" nor "banal."[19] Ken may be a less skilful practitioner than Dryden or Cowley, but he has his niche in the gallery of neoclassical verse.

In the last resort neoclassical verse depends on the precision and scope of the single word; the word must be precise enough to give colour and shape, and have the scope of generalised and accepted meaning. Then these single words must be put together to form a striking and tasteful ensemble. One of the characteristics of the neoclassicists is their tendency to form lists or brief strings of these single words, in an attempt to be as concisely inclusive as possible. Ken employed this technique, but he was also aware of its source in the Renaissance practice of rhetorical enumeration.

In his devotional poetry Ken used the technique of rhetorical enumeration as a shorthand to interpret spiritual experience. Thus, addressing Christ, he writes:

To me be Water, Oil, Fire, Wind,
To cleanse, oint, warm, and wing my mind.[20]

Here the double list corresponds exactly noun to verb. In another lyric there is an equally exact, though less immediately obvious, series of corresponding antitheses, where each of the eight terms gains in precision by being defined against its opposite:

From Closet, Reading, Temple, Altar, I
Back to the world in a few minutes fly,
Noise, Converse, Business, and my Station there,
Are apt to rifle all I gain by prayer.[21]

This reduction of the activities of religious and social life to the poetic diction of neoclassical personifications is an interesting example of the way in which Metaphysical techniques, based on the figures of Renaissance rhetoric, were being simplified, fixed and stereotyped. As such they became an important ingredient in the satirical couplets of Augustan poets.

Ken used the enumeration of single words in an idiom close to that of Pope when he wrote: "Dice, Tavern, Stews, Balls, Evening

[18] *Ibid.*, II, 118–19.
[19] Rice, p. 182.
[20] "Jesus Love Preserved," Ken, I, 500.
[21] "Desire," Ken, I, 523.

Tour and Stage."[22] And yet on the same page we find a similar line written in quasi-devotional idiom: "His Conscience, Credit, Time, Purse, Health to waste." Pope was to develop this technique into a far subtler and more refined weapon of satire and abuse. For Ken the technique remained a tool to draw a crude contrast in morality, though there is a touch of sophisticated mockery in his reference to the "language of eye, look and fan."[23]

In assessing Ken's contribution to neoclassical verse, we should rather consider, as a companion piece to his attack on latitudinarianism, the equivalent passage in "Hymnotheo." This is the rumbustious catalogue of Restoration vices suitable as butts for the religious-minded satirist. It runs as follows:

Time serving Changeling, Machiavellian Fourb,
Proud Schismatics, who holy Church disturb;
The brutish Glutton, and the drunken Sot;
Vile Lechers, who with Strumpets stink and rot;
Affected Gallants, and the squandering Heir,
The hectoring Bravoes, who the Cowards scare;
The rich starved Miser, and the churlish Hog;
The cozening Gamester, who a die can cog;
The Sensualist in intermundian ease;
Poets obscene the gaudy mob to please;
The fawning Courtier kissing great men's feet,
The wild Enthusiast, the religious cheat;
Cursed Heretics who saving truth deny;
The philosophic Fops who God defy;
Haughty Contemners of the good and wise,
The smooth tongued Villain with enchanting lies;
The lewd Monk, wanton Nun, licentious Priest;
Prelates who starve their flocks themselves to feast;
All Satan's spies, and doubly damned decoys,
Whom to tempt others, daily he employs;
These and a thousand humours more they hit,
With an insulting, and satiric wit.[24]

So it is not entirely true to say that Ken writes like one "who has lived on into times which nourish neither his thought nor his art."[25] In these twin passages from his two major epics, there is a harmonious combination of thought and technique, spirit and style, in the dominant literary idiom of his time, the heroic couplet.

[22] "Hymnotheo," Ken, III, 63.
[23] "Psyche," Ken, IV, 237.
[24] Ken, III, 278. Fourb = cheat, impostor (*OED*). To cog a die = fraudulently to control the fall of the dice (*OED*).

That Ken exploited his neoclassical vein with so much mediocrity in all but these key passages is indeed unfortunate. But it must not be forgotten that Ken held a higher view of poetry than the neoclassical aesthetic could satisfy:

> Of all the gifts which heaven designed
> To hallow and adorn the mind,
> Sweet Poetry has suffered most,
> By bards from the infernal coast,
> Who in her beauteous visage spit
> The putrefaction of their wit.[26]

Ken's verse is primarily marked by an attempt to protect the sweet poetry of the devotional Metaphysicals from the ravages of neoclassical wit.

[25] Fairchild, I, 105.
[26] "Urania," Ken, IV, 475.

CHAPTER FIVE

THE METAPHYSICAL TRADITION

"Edmund" and "Hymnotheo" are the only two of Ken's poems in which neoclassicism predominates. In these epics the Metaphysical tradition is present chiefly in the form of 17th century spiritual machinery. Ken's lyric epics on the other hand – "Christophil," "Psyche," "Sion" and "Urania" – have a fairly persistent Metaphysical strain running through them, and are written in a variety of metres. These lyric epics are much nearer in diction and tone to the strongly Metaphysical sequences of lyrics which constitute "Songs to Jesus" in volume one, "Hymns on the Attributes of God" in volume two, "Anodynes" in volume three, and "Preparatives for Death" in volume four.

Clearly the Metaphysical tradition survived longer in the religious lyric than in any other form of poetry. Even if one can denigrate Ken *qua* epic writer for being "but a weak follower of Cowley," there is less justice in attacking him *qua* lyricist for being "but a weak follower of Herbert."[1] The followers of Cowley were many and uniformly mediocre; the followers of Herbert were few and rare. Indeed noone, Edward Taylor always excepted, was so consistently writing adequate Metaphysical lyrics in the 1690s as was Ken; and some have claimed that the "Anodynes" were written as late as 1710–1711.[2] Fragments of a Metaphysical tradition can be identified in certain religious poets of the 18th century, in Watts for example, but Ken is the last English poet to belong centrally to this tradition.

As such he is of course an anachronism. In his life as well as his devotional lyricism he belongs to another age. Not only did he possess Donne's gold signet ring, handed down to him by Izaac Walton;[3] he

[1] Plumptre, II, 232.
[2] *Ibid.*, II, 199.
[3] *Ibid.*, I, 20.

also sang to his lute before dressing in the morning,[4] and travelled with his shroud in his portmanteau.[5] Correspondingly, what is remarkable in his verse is not its pale reflection of Herbert, but the strength of its Metaphysical qualities. These are not wholly surrendered in their contact with the mannerisms and clichés of poetic diction, and it is instructive to examine their fortunes in an age which can barely sustain them.

A look at three of Ken's poems on death will provide a preliminary indication of the nature and strength of the Metaphysical tradition in the religious lyric of the 1690s. In "Dying to the World," in spite of the didactic title, there is the authentic Donne-like tone, the quaintly moving argument:

> Death, when for me you are designed,
> But little work in me you'll find.
>
> . . . .
>
> Death, when you shall approach my head,
> You'll nothing see but what is dead.[6]

The tone may be derivative and the execution formal, but the waning of the middle ages goes on. 17th century death is still with us, strong enough to draw men into serious argument. Death is a busy worker; wit is required to fend him off. We are far from the indulgence of the 18th century graveyard school.

But Ken uses other weapons than Metaphysical wit to deal with death. In "The Soul Polluted in the Body," the old running sore of death, as described by Shakespeare, Raleigh and Webster, is cicatrised into the mannerism of an emblem. The stink and rot of early 17th century physical detail are fumigated, and the way lies open for the indulgence of the 18th century graveyard poets:

> See on my lids the maggots lie,
> And eat the apple of my eye,
> A serpent at my mouth is hung,
> And greedily devours my tongue,
> Worms gorge themselves in every part,
> An odious toad there gnaws my heart.[7]

Ken here aligns himself with the authors of emblem-books, whose work, after Quarles, facilitated the transition from Metaphysical to

4 William Hawkins, p. 5 and Plumptre, II, 227
5 Plumptre, II, 202.
6 Ken, IV, 145–6.
7 Ken, IV, 154.

Augustan, first by moralising, then by aestheticising material which had been treated with a combination of high seriousness and quaint wit. The emphasis switches from the rhetorically persuasive declamation to the aesthetically pleasing picture. The rhetorical enumeration of the parts of the body, which forms the structure of this passage, does not so much pursue the amplification of argument, as Marvell does with sophisticated irony in "To his Coy Mistress," but rather fills in the emblem with all its joints. And yet the emblem-books themselves belonged to the 17th century, and Ken is transitional in the same way.

The measure of his attachment to the consciousness which nourished Metaphysical poetry can be seen in "The Soul Hovering over our Ashes." In an age when the aesthetics of infinity were encouraging the flight of the soul through the virgin lands of space, Ken shuns the sublime aspirations of the Pindaric, and has his soul make "a reverence to its ruins":

Descend a while and view my urn,
See how my limbs to ashes turn;
Though Heaven your tears may stop,
Yet you a sigh may drop,
My dust to meet your sigh will rise,
And with your yearnings sympathise.

Your wings o'er my cold atoms spread,
Brooding kind heat upon them dead.
. . . .
Re-enter your old friend.[8]

Donne and Webster were "much possessed by death, / And saw the skull beneath the skin."[9] At the end of the century Ken still works in this tradition, using the separation of soul and body to coin the idiom of Metaphysical wit. These three poems then suggest lines along which to identify the Metaphysical tradition in Ken. But they also suggest ways in which this tradition disintegrated, through the exigencies of didacticism, the mannerisms of decadence, and the inroads made by the contemporary Enlightenment consciousness.

As corroboration of Ken's position as a poet, and as an introduction to an analysis of that position, mention should be made of his prose style. If more of Ken's sermons were extant, there is little doubt that

[8] Ken, IV, 131–3.
[9] T. S. Eliot, "Whispers of Immortality," in *Collected Poems 1909–35* (London: Faber and Faber, 1956), p. 53.

he would occupy an important place in the history of English prose. The quality of writing in the few sermons we have is way above anything he was capable of as a poet. Much has been made of the development of the 17th century sermon, in which the slow but sure movement from Renaissance to Augustan can be traced in the works of Donne, Andrewes, Taylor, South, Barrow and Tillotson. Ken offers an interesting example of a preacher whose style is rooted in the age of Donne and Andrewes, and yet has the civilised smoothness of Tillotson. He thus exemplifies, perhaps more strikingly than Taylor or South, the two-headed nature of much 17th century prose, at once baroque and polite, Metaphysical and Augustan.

The source of Ken's prose style, and its constant infrastructure whatever the surface embroidery, lies in the simplicity and richness of Biblical rhetoric. This gives a style which is neither plain nor baroque. With the 1611 translation gaining acceptance, this style became every able preacher's Parnassian:

> O Sirs, the harvest of souls at this time is great: the prebends are many, the priests are many, the deans are many – the labourers are few: shall I pray the Lord of the harvest to turn you out, and send forth labourers into His harvest?[10]

It is unfortunate that the early 17th century did not develop an equally resistant Parnassian for its poetry; as it was this was left to neoclassicism, and the Metaphysicals shone brilliantly if fitfully without the sustenance of a consciously practised aesthetic.

Elaborations on this prose Parnassian were manifold. Three at least can be identified in Ken. Each provides evidence that Ken contributed to the development from baroque to polite in prose as well as in verse. Thus he was able to refine and civilise the heavy latinate constructions beloved of the Ciceronians from Hooker to Milton; in Ken's hands such constructions took on the weightless ease of a polite compliment:

> I know not how to call it, but there is a meltingness of disposition and affectionateness of devotion, an easy sensibility, an industrious alacrity, a languishing ardour, in piety, peculiar to the sex, which naturally renders them subjects more pliable to the divine grace than men commonly are.[11]

The subject-matter – piety, and not, as for Hooker and Milton, polemic – helps, but Ken does not avoid or eliminate the Ciceronian; he cherishes and assimilates it.

[10] *Ichabod*, in Ken, *Prose Works*, p. 47.
[11] "Funeral Sermon on Lady Maynard," in *ibid.*, p. 62.

A second elaboration can be seen in Ken's taste for a heavily stylised antithetical rhetoric. One passage from *Ichabod* is particularly striking in this respect. Ken attacks those Presbyterians and Independents who had refused the accommodation offered them by the moderate Anglicans before the establishment of the Commonwealth, and who had nevertheless returned to the fold at the Restoration:

Ah, blessed Hammond, thou didst write rationally; excellent Gauden, thou didst persuade powerfully; devout Taylor, thou didst urge pathetically; honest Nicholson, thou didst answer satisfactorily; solid Sanderson, thou didst state clearly; holy Usher and Hall, you did offer moderately, heartily and learnedly. But who, O ye worthies! believed your report? Who would hear you? Who was convinced by you? The King is restored, I flourish, and dispose of all preferments, and my converts are innumerable.[12]

The recourse to alliteration and assonance – the first six parallelisms governed by r, p, t, n, s, and h, respectively – is as systematic as in many of his couplets. Such stylised techniques were possible in prose, but needed a lot of refinement if they were to suit the idiom of the couplet. In this passage they suit the rhetorical scheme, which is designed to pour heavy scorn on the innumerable converts, and give high praise to the select heroes. The staccato notes are so nicely balanced that they build up a smooth tone, such as Andrewes, with his mania for staccato, rarely achieves.

A third elaboration on preaching Parnassian can be seen in Ken's development of a civilised lyricism. The Biblical source of the Song of Solomon offered a theme that was to remain popular into the early years of the 18th century. Its refinement was an important factor in the survival of Metaphysical elements in religious lyricism long after they had disappeared in other kinds of poetry. Ken retains the richness and syntax of early 17th century prose, but allows his taste for lyricism to smooth out the gothic edges of 17th century typology:

Beauty gratifies only our outward sense; it is a mixture of colour, and figure, and feature, and parts, all in due proportion and symmetry; or indeed it is a well-shaped frame of dust and ashes, beloved by fond men only, who, like the most stupid of idolaters, worship the bare statue, without regard to the deity there enshrined: but Grace is a confluence of all attractives, which approves itself to our own most deliberate judgments, and is beloved by God. Do but imagine you were in the Spouse's garden, where, when the south wind blows, the several spices and gums, the spikenard and the cinnamon, the frankincense and myrrh send forth their various

[12] *Ichabod*, in *ibid.*, p. 25. For notes on Hammond, Gauden, Taylor, Nicholson, Sanderson, Ussher and Hall, see Appendix I.

smells... As a jewel of gold in a swine's snout, which is hung there on purpose to be defiled, to be rolled in filth and mire and is one of the most notorious and ugly incongruities in the world; such a kind of absurdity, if you will believe Solomon, is a fair woman without discretion.[13]

Many of Ken's lyrics follow a similar pattern and mood, but never in verse does he achieve the mastery of syntax that characterises his prose. The moral exposition proper to prose becomes an insistent didacticism that sullies the spirit of his lyrics.

The important thing in Ken's prose is its roots, which go back to Donne and Andrewes. At times Ken appears remarkably close to Andrewes in his manner of textual preaching:

If then you would learn Daniel's secret, that powerful inflammative and preservative of love, which Daniel had, and which made him, according to the text, understood in a passive sense, a man greatly beloved: take the very same expression in an active sense, and then you have it; he did greatly love, and therefore he was greatly beloved: that was all the court-cunning, all the philtre that Daniel had. It is love that most naturally attracts love; and from this love he is called, "a man of desires"; of desires for the glory of God, and for the welfare of King and people; still I am short: he was a man full of desires; so full that he was made up of desires, he was all desires; for so the original emphatically styles him, "thou art desires" (Dan. ix. 23).[14]

It was Andrewes who perfected this type of grammatical acrobatics around the exposition of a text; an arabesque is gradually built up as the full meaning emerges under grammatical analysis. Straight out of Andrewes also is the insistent repetition of the key word, and the subsuming of all that has been wound out of the text back into the text at the conclusion. Ken preached this sermon in 1685, which helps account for the survival of a Metaphysical style in his verse written even later. Tillotson was still a pioneer in modernising the prose style of sermons, when he replaced Sancroft as Archbishop of Canterbury. Sancroft, whose *Occasional Sermons* were published in 1694, was still preaching in the style of Andrewes.[15] Ken's style is nearer to Tillotson's than Sancroft's was, but like Sancroft's it belongs to the earlier tradition. Tillotson's kindred spirit, Gilbert Burnet, acknowledges this when he notes that Ken "had a very edifying way of preaching, but it was more apt to move the passions than to instruct,

[13] "Funeral Sermon on Lady Maynard," in *ibid.*, pp. 63, 64.

[14] "1685 Sermon," in *ibid.*, pp. 82–3.

[15] See L. G. Locke, p. 126. William Sancroft (1617–93) was deprived of his archbishopric in 1689. A disciple of Andrewes and Laud, he joined in the preparations for the consecration of new non-juring bishops, and in 1691 delegated his authority to William Lloyd, the deprived Bishop of Norwich. *DNB*

so that his sermons were rather beautiful than solid, yet his way in them was very taking."[16] From Burnet this is indeed high praise. Ken's imperviousness to the Baconian linguistic reforms of the Royal Society is in fact the saving grace of both his prose and his verse.

Two traces of the Metaphysical mood to be found in Ken's verse are the sense of precise local situation, and the interpretation of nature as a divine hieroglyph. Thus Ken can say in a poem which analyses his sleeplessness, "I feel my watch," and his editor can add in a footnote – the only one in four long volumes –, "His watch was purposely so contrived as that he could by his finger discover the time, to half a quarter of an hour."[17] Without arguing that the footnote improves the poem, it is true to say that this little physical detail helps Ken to resist the ever-present threat of poetic diction. Such precision of detail does not necessarily raise the quality of the verse. The "Anodynes" get along quite well without any indication of the particular bodily pains endured, and the avowal, after eighty pages of grappling with suffering, that "Thou gracious God, me to reform, / My flesh with colic pains didst storm,"[18] adds nothing to the poetic value or otherwise of the meditations. Again, the information that "My friends, who with me sympathise, / To opium warmly me advise,"[19] appears as a strangely gratuitous piece of autobiographical detail. Nevertheless, though this sense of precise local situation is badly integrated, it is difficult to wish it omitted.

At times indeed, the precision appears less gratuitous. Thus the mention of stomach, feet and nerves at the end of "The Soul Polluted in the Body" invigorates the rather stale military imagery of "recruits" and "reserves":

> My stomach fails, I can no more
> With fresh recruits my strength restore,
> My feet begin to freeze, my flaccid nerves
> Have for their craving drains no brisk reserves.[20]

And in "Watch and Pray" the vision that is described has body, because it takes place in a particular spot and at a particular hour:

[16] Gilbert Burnet, *History of My Own Time*, ed. O. Airy (2 vols.; Oxford: Clarendon Press, 1897–1900), II, 433. Quoted in Plumptre, I, 179.
[17] "Anodynes," Ken, III, 396.
[18] Ken, III, 470.
[19] Ken, III, 397.
[20] Ken, IV, 155–6.

It chanced, just as the full-checked Moon
Reached her nocturnal noon,
Into a garden shade withdrew,
Heaven undistractedly to view,
And as to God my prayer took flight,
I saw a very formidable sight.

On a pale horse I Death descried.[21]

The precise detail allows the last line of the first verse to be matter-of-fact and striking, instead of vague and bathetic.

Perhaps Ken's most powerful evocation of precise situation is his vision of the miser:

I saw this day a miser old,
Receive and count a bag of gold,
His spectacles he cleared,
And on his nostrils reared,
Then moved his table towards the light,
To gain an unobstructed sight.[22]

Such observation of detail owes nothing to the Metaphysical tradition. As objective realism, it belongs, if anywhere, to the line of character-writing which runs through the 17th century. It forms part of a poem intended as a meditation preparative to death. It is thus the purpose rather than the performance which belongs to the Metaphysical tradition. Such eclecticism suggests that no one way of writing poetry dominates in Ken's work, and that his Metaphysical roots lie elsewhere than in the precise detail of localised situation.

A Metaphysical mood, however poorly exploited, can be detected in Ken's use of the microcosm and his treatment of nature as a divine hieroglyph. On one occasion the microcosmic reference is part of a periphrasis, which manages to take two couplets to say "I woke up":

The soul which all night long its motions ceased,
Sun of the little world brake from its east,
And raised by these sweet notes, the mists dispelled,
Which in deep silence had the senses held.[23]

The expression is otiose and the microcosm is handled with conscious prettiness rather than used to discover truth. The heavy tread of the verse however does not suggest that Ken intended to make fun of the concept of microcosm. And in the "Anodynes," he shows that he takes the concept quite seriously, and can use it to create a more

21 Ken, IV, 92.
22 "The Miser," Ken, IV, 3–4.
23 "Hymnotheo," Ken, III, 316.

genuinely Metaphysical mood, in spite of a diction that is strongly emblematic:

> When painted flames within me pent,
> Rack all my nerves to force a vent,
> Unable to transpire,
> Enrage my inward fire;
> Raise by compression dolorous groans,
> And a tremendous earthquake in my bones.[24]

This is a perfect example of the late Metaphysical style, stilted perhaps, but saved from the decadence of preciosity by the emblematic idiom in which it is cast. The Metaphysical style was able to survive so long in religious poetry, because it fell back on a crude poetic diction of its own. Ken must nevertheless be one of the last devotional poets to make serious use of the microcosm.

Nature as the divine hieroglyph figures prominently in the poetry of Fane,[25] Marvell and Vaughan. Cowley is usually considered to be the last to "echo this neoplatonic or Hermetic sentiment," which in the previous generation had been a method of discovering and displaying truth, rather than a feeling "concerning the actual presence of God in the creation."[26] Ken, like the Metaphysicals, and unlike Cowley, who in this matter was a pioneer of the modern consciousness, was not interested in drawing sentiments from nature. He was still able, a generation after the death of Cowley, to use nature as a divine hieroglyph. What betrays Ken's lateness is his manner of employing this tradition as if it were an isolated literary embellishment, cut off from the sustenance of living thought.

Ken's chunks of divine hieroglyph are to be found in the poetically unintegrated forms of a protracted simile, lengthy emblematic description, and moral anatomy. The protracted simile sees a pair of lovers as

> Male and female palms, whose roots conjoin,
> Whose bows to a perpetual kiss incline;
> Their shady locks into each other wreath,
> Their mutual sweets into each other breathe;
> Their morning dew into each other drop,
> Both feel the wound, if you should either crop.[27]

[24] Ken, III, 397.
[25] Mildmay Fane (d. 1666) was the author of *Otia Sacra* (1648).
[26] M. Rostvig, *The Happy Man: Studies in the Metamorphoses of a Classical Ideal* (2 vols.; "Oslo Studies in English," Nos. 2 and 7; Oslo: Akademisk Forlag; Oxford: Blackwell, 1954–8), I, 305–6.
[27] "Edmund," Ken, II, 259.

Of course this is a metaphorical description, but it makes no sense if it does not express a serious belief in the realities of vegetable love. The vegetable world corresponds to the little world of man, and provides a means of projecting the limited possibilities of eroticism onto a perspective "vaster than empires."[28] As such, this represents an authentic technique of Metaphysical poetry, however less skilfully managed by Ken than by Marvell.

Ken's most striking use of lengthy emblematic description occurs in two passages, both designed to evoke an idealised landscape with prelapsarian vegetation. The first employs the contemporary catalogue of minerals to describe New Jerusalem. The Biblical account of the Heavenly City is embellished with all the colours known to 17th century mineralogists. These were almost as manifold as those revealed to the 18th century physico-theological poets who had read Newton's *Optics*:

With that the prince she to a gallery led,
Where with enamouring sights his eyes were fed;
The floor with gold was curiously enwrought,
From Parvaim, Havilah, and Ophir brought;
Black Sardins there, and Rubies fiery red,
The Chrysopass with golden spots bespread;
The Hyacinth of violacean hue,
The purple Amethyst, and Sapphire blue;
Gold Chrysolite, the Pearl unspotted white,
Opal and Iris of mixed coloured light;
The yellow Topaz, and the Emerald green;
All gems which in the pectoral were seen,
Or which illustrious Solomon bedecked,
Or in New Salem brightest rays reflect;
And Diamonds which with different waters shined,
Were on the walls in rare mosaic joined.[29]

Ken was not old-fashioned in his taste for precious stones; nor was he following a purely literary convention. His younger contemporary, the scientist John Ray, meditated on this theme with equal assiduity:

In stones which one would think were a neglected genus, what variety? What beauty and elegancy? What constancy in their temper and consistency, in their figures and colours? The qualities I shall instance in are first colour, which in some of them is most lively, sparkling, and beautiful. The Carbuncle or Rubine shining with red, the Sapphire with blue, the

[28] See Marvell, "To his coy mistress."
[29] "Edmund," Ken, II, 163.

Emerald with green, the Topaz or Chrysolite of the ancients with a yellow or gold colour, the Amethyst as it were tinctured with wine, the Opal varying its colours like changeable taffety, as it is diversely exposed to the light.[30]

Precious stones were no more neglected by poets in the 17th century than the colours of the rainbow were by poets in the 18th century.

The second passage describes the Garden of Eden in the convention that produced Marvell's "Garden," though in Ken's hands the moral is more important than the mood, and suggests temperance rather than ecstasy:

The bowing fruits strove which should first be cropped,
Bees without stings pure virgin honey dropped;
Sweet rosebuds on unprickled bushes blew.
. . . .
Transporting sights around them charm their eyes,
Which joined, up to transporting landskips rise;
Till admiration all the soul o'erflows,
And from admiring poetry arose.
. . . .
No tree was then more bulky than the vine,
Needing no prop, on which it should recline;
Till by intemperance debased it joined
To other trees, and on supporters twined,
To teach fallen men who surfeit on its juice,
The weakness they contract by its abuse.[31]

The pious conclusion should not obscure the hieroglyphic content of the passage. There is for example an interesting contrast with the post-lapsarian palms in the protracted simile from "Edmund" – "both feel the wound if you should either crop"; whereas before the Fall, "the bowing fruits strove which should first be cropped." Ken does not insist on the microcosmic correspondences of his vegetation, but they are inevitably implied, latent through the weight of long tradition. Thus the "bowing fruits" and the "vine needing no prop" cannot be separated from the traditional symbolism, such as is used by Marvell. This sort of symbolism is inseparable from the mood of Metaphysical poetry, and Ken is repeating unimaginatively material

[30] John Ray, *The Wisdom of God Manifested in the Works of the Creation* (London, 1691), p. 67.

[31] "Hymnotheo," Ken, III, 318, 323.

which Marvell wove into some of the finest poetry the 17th century produced.[32]

In a passage of moral anatomy Ken applies the divine hieroglyph to the microcosm. Unfortunately the didacticism stifles any Metaphysical play on the correspondence between human physiology – "atom," "breast," "gust" – and the mineral world – "stone," "dust":

All want of Man, the noble thinking part,
Anatomise them, and you'll find no heart;
A stone in every breast that place supplies,
And entrance to true wisdom still denies;
Which, were it in a mortar brayed to dust,
Each atom would retain its sensual gust.[33]

The diction is stilted and lame. Yet the very idea of anatomy kept in its primarily physiological sense, and the very tone of "you'll find no heart" – a moral conclusion from a physical premiss –, belong to the Metaphysical tradition.

Of various other Metaphysical evident in Ken's verse, one is his use of the compass as an image. The Metaphysical poets were particularly attracted to the mathematician's compasses, from which they drew many an argument and proved many a point. Ken too was able to use a conceit to further a logical argument. But he was also drawn to the mariner's compass, which could serve as an aid to devotion when applied to the microcosm of introspective analysis.

The correspondence between the elements of nature and the human anatomy is made possible by the compass conceit when Ken writes:

Like various Winds, my circling Pains
Fly all the compass of my veins.[34]

Another compass conceit provides a valid theological argument to strengthen the poet's devotion:

God is the centre of my mind.
. . . .
Yet oft I find a scruple start,
How God is centre of my heart;
The centre we a point esteem,
Lines thither from the compass stream,

[32] See Marvell, "The Garden," where the theology of the Fall is metamorphosed into a paradise of Platonic indulgence. Cf. also "Appleton House," esp. line 520. Andrew Marvell, *Poems and Letters*, ed. H. M. Margoliouth (2 vols.; Oxford: Clarendon Press, 1927), I, 49, 75.
[33] "Hymnotheo," Ken, III, 191.
[34] "Anodynes," Ken, III, 429.

But godhead is immense,
God is both centre and circumference.[35]

The conclusion is commonplace, but the argument is Metaphysical and would appear a trite trick to an Augustan. In fact the argument is not a piece of pure cerebral scholasticism, because Ken implies that he has improved it from experience. When he returns to this theme in another place, he writes:

O 'tis a truth that I have often tried,
That souls not where they live, but love, abide.
. . . .
Thou art my love's true centre, out of thee
My love alive can no one moment be.
Souls in chaste love a like propension find,
And live in transmigrations of the mind.[36]

The compass conceit has dissolved; assertion takes the place of argument. And yet there is an element of Metaphysical structure in the veiled image of a magnetic force. The word "centre" and "propension" conceal some sort of compass figure, and it is the logic of this implied conceit which develops the quaint and utterly Metaphysical reference to "transmigrations of the mind." This fusion of logic and conceit is certainly one of the most characteristic techniques of the Metaphysical poet.

Ken then is not wholly oblivious to the chief tenet of Renaissance aesthetics, the integration of logical argument and rhetorical amplification into the structure of poetry. At one point he makes a sally into the logical basis of ontology, using the technical terms from the textbooks, as Donne and Lord Herbert were wont to do:

A vapour ere dissolved in air,
A flower ere ceasing to look fair,
A sleep, a dream, ere they expire,
Some short duration still require;
But life fleets rather than abides,
Away in half a second slides.

Methinks when death I call to mind,
Life might be easily defined;
Death's a privation of our all,
Life then we should fruition call:

35 "Psyche," Ken, IV, 203.
36 "Edmund," Ken, II, 253.

Yet nothing we to life allow,
But the fruition of this now.[37]

"Duration," "require," "privation," "fruition," "allow" – these are technical terms with specialised philosophical meanings; they are terms used in logical analysis, and Ken is able to use them as the bones of his poem. The flesh he provides in the form of rhetorical amplification drawn from examples contained in these same textbooks. Hence "vapour," "flower," "sleep," "dream," "life," "death" – all are related to the pursuit of a definition. Of such stuff was the Metaphysical lyric made.

In one of Ken's most Metaphysical moments, logically constructed hypotheses are used to account for the apparent lateness of the sun's rising:

Pain keeps me waking in the night,
I longing lie for morning light;
Methinks the sluggish sun,
Forgets he this day's course must run.
. . . .
Sure some new spots your face besmear,
And you're ashamed to reappear.
. . . .
Or night your rising now restrains,
Till it the ten degrees regains
It lost when back you went,
And the sick king learned heaven's intent;
Assured of supplemental years,
By your remeasuring of the spheres.[38]

The ability to inform hypothetical arguments with a serious lyrical wit is one of the more complicated characteristics of Metaphysical poetry. Donne, in "The Sunne Rising," approached his subject with a similar tone and like arguments, though aimed to demonstrate an opposite conclusion. It is not often that Ken avoids the pitfalls of this technique; his "sluggish sun" threatens to become a pathetic fallacy,

[37] "Life," Ken, IV, 40. Cf. Donne's similar use of textbook categories in his "Nocturnal upon St Lucy's Day":

"Were I a man, that I were one,
I needs must know; I should prefer,
If I were any beast,
Some ends, some means; Yea plants, yea stones detest,
And love; All, all some properties invest."

John Donne, *Complete Poems and Selected Prose*, ed. J. Hayward (London: Nonesuch Press, 1955), pp. 32–3.

[38] "Anodynes," Ken, III, 395–6.

but this is held off by the logical precision of argument geared to the dominant tone of pain.

If the logic of the conceit is the principal characteristic of Metaphysical poetry, one of its most important by-products is the technique of introspective analysis. This was encouraged by the habit of logic and the potentialities of the microcosm. On the whole the Enlightenment poets discarded the techniques of introspection and preferred to investigate the macrocosm. Ken, as we have seen, is conspicuous in his failure to make much of the aesthetics of infinity. In practising the aesthetics of the microcosm he is rather more successful.

In the following signal example introspection and logical conceit combine to make poetry in the manner of Herbert:

Let others sail the world about,
To find strange countries out,
A land unknown I have within,
Inhabited by sin,
Which from my intellectual view,
Longtime itself withdrew.

My thought had often made assay,
Its limits to survey,
But still it found out something new,
Which ne'er before I knew,
And though I launched my thought again,
It voyage made in vain.

It glides away like floating isles,
My anchor it beguiles,
Worse monsters there excite my dread,
Than Africk ever bred,
Proud Babel's ruins never bore,
Such a mis-shapen store.

To God I then my self applied,
That he my course would guide;
Kind heaven a compass to me gave,
To steer me in the wave,
And coasting round the moving sands,
My thought upon it lands.

It was my heart I searched, unknown
To all but God alone;
It was by God's all gracious aid,
I my discoveries made,

His law my needle, in straight line,
Turned to the pole divine.

With that I o'er the region strayed,
It was of labyrinths made,
And I when disengaged from one,
Into another run.
When their amusements me aggrieved,
My needle me relieved.[39]

This passage is quoted in full because it represents Ken's most sustained piece of devotional lyricism. The quality that raises it above the mediocre Parnassian in which it is cast is distinctly if not strikingly Metaphysical.

The rhythm and diction owe nearly everything to the tradition in which Herbert writes, and it is remarkable that Herbert's idiom suits Ken so well. What is even more remarkable is that so late in the 17th century a devotional poet can avoid the open country of the sublime. Ken is still nourished by what is little and difficult, by the nice intricacies of conscience and the subtle hints of grace, qualities which combine so often to give movement and body to Herbert's verse. Ken even manages the dramatic element, registering the shifts of mood as conscience and grace move to their meeting. The beginning of the fifth verse, with its quaint discovery, invites comparison with the conclusion of "Carrion Comfort" by G. M. Hopkins. Where Ken's wistful search for God ends in a placid discovery of his own heart, Hopkins' agonising introspection becomes a "no-manfathomed" struggle with God. Where the Metaphysical style cultivates the discovery of spiritual security, the Romantic style cultivates the revelation of bottomless insecurity. Ken's control over his imagery matches the cool collected experience he describes. "Africk's monsters" and "Babel's ruins" are sober metaphors, unusually precise and apt. They help to make the word "discoveries" a delightfully balanced ambiguity, by giving an extra bit of geographical ballast to the primary weight of moral revelation. When the spiritual pilgrimage is complete, its efficacy is tested by means of the compass, and the proof the conceit offers is quietly affirmed: "My needle me relieved."

The ability to turn introspection into poetry was thus nourished by the Metaphysical tradition, and after Ken there was no effective poetry of introspection until Wordsworth. Ken was content to be "coasting round the moving sands" of his consciousness; moving or

39 "Psyche," Ken, IV, 193–4.

not, there was at least a coast to trace. The Enlightenment poets, Edward Young first and foremost, had nothing to trace as they floated sublimely on the high seas of infinity. This could not but harm the religious lyric. The spirit of the age in which Ken wrote could afford to be against coasting, both geographically and spiritually. The perfected precision of the new loadstone on the one hand, and the watertight evidences of Enlightenment religion on the other, made for plain sailing on the open sea.

Locke had claimed: "He that first discovered the use of the compass did more for the supplying and increase of useful commodities, than those who built workhouses."[40] And Ray had set the tone of the 1690s with his encomium on the loadstone:

> Its verticity and direction to the poles of the earth is of later invention; which of how infinite advantage it hath been to these two or three last ages, the great improvement of navigation and advancement of trade and commerce by rendering the remotest countries easily accessible, the noble discovery of a vast continent or new world, besides a multitude of unknown kingdoms and islands, the resolving experimentally those ancient problems of the spherical roundness of the earth; of the being of Antipodes, of the habitableness of the torrid zone and the rendering the whole terraqueous globe circumnavigable, do abundantly demonstrate; whereas formerly they were wont to coast it, and creep along the shores, scarce daring to venture out of the ken of land.[41]

Ken and the Metaphysicals had rifled this material for their conceits, and discovered invaluable correspondences between the geographical and spiritual worlds. The vein was more or less exhausted by the time Ken came to write in "Edmund":

> Though to the utmost point of the Arctic Pole,
> I run my course to find that lovely soul,
> My love has force to plough those stormy seas,
> And fire, the icy mountains to unfreeze:
> Were she a native of the torrid zone,
> I'd thither take a voyage from my throne;
> The sun's bright beams put out a feeble fire,
> And at my flame, those fervours would expire.
> Should all the blasts which blow the compass round,
> Confederate, my feeble bark to drownd,
> Yet my propensions in her love combined,
> Would fill the sails, and stem the adverse wind.[42]

[40] Quoted in Samuel Johnson, *A Dictionary of the English Language* (2 vols.; 6th ed., London: Rivington, 1785), "Compass" 9.

[41] Ray, p. 70.

[42] Ken, II, 243–4.

Ken almost manages to give new life to the worn-out material. On the whole however, his age was no longer interested in the traffic of wit and introspection, but only in the "useful commodities" of trade and commerce.

A view of Ken's place in the Metaphysical tradition would be incomplete without reference to the spiritual machinery to be found in his epics. In any late 17th century poet who had an interest in the structure and techniques of epic poetry, one would expect to find signs of stress and incongruity, due to the inability of the heroic poem to adapt itself to a scientific age; one would expect that some sort of comparison to Milton would be called for. But Ken is oblivious to such problems, his epics are without structure, and there is an absence of technical resources. There is however some action; and there are spiritual and immaterial beings who take part in the action. At such moments it is possible to talk of the incongruity and absurdity of Ken's spiritual machinery.

Angels, whose serious existence in the religious lyric was not threatened until well into the 18th century, were clearly no longer fit to take part in an epic without making themselves look ridiculous.[43] In the lyric direct address to an angel was still possible, and Ken could speak to his guardian spirit, as the Metaphysicals were wont to do, cajolingly and devoutly:

> My love in this shall yours outdo,
> 'Twill be the tenderer of the two.[44]

But in heroic couplets Ken's angels appear out of their element, pinned down like captured butterflies, slightly absurd, almost comic. Thus Ken writes of his

> Guardian, who a while to heaven had flown,
> To sing his course at the tribunal throne.[45]

Ken seems here to have abandoned the grave wit of the Metaphysicals, and moved towards the gay levity of the opening of Byron's *Vision of Judgment.*

[43] In the middle of the 18th century Henry Brooke still takes angels seriously, though his treatment of them lacks Miltonic sublimity. He writes of "angelic shapes that wing th'etherial space," and then proceeds to murder them by dissection, defining them as

> "Nor spirit all – nor yet corporeal frame;
> Than one, more dense – than t'other, more refined;
> If spirit, organised – if matter, mind."

Universal Beauty, I, 197–202 in Chalmers, XVII, 339.

[44] "On the Circumcision," Ken, I, 216.

[45] "Resignation of Jesus," Ken, I, 502.

In his epics Ken's angels lose their reality and become pious pictures clad in Sunday School raiment:

> On their unbodied spirits both did wear
> Extemporaneous vehicles of air,
> One ruby bright, the other pearl-like pale,
> The pearl the female was, the ruby male.[46]

Ken does nothing to render palatable his confusion between matter and spirit; he will have his heroic action, and he will have his immaterial beings. When these beings meet in battle, the result is:

> Thus partly by antipathies they fought,
> And stabbed each other through and through with thought.[47]

And to picture their suffering, extension is necessary:

> Thus shrivelled spirits in hard crystal pent,
> Racked by contraction, raving roared for vent.[48]

When the fighting is over, we hear of spirits who "long to gain an immaterial kiss."[49] Some of them have their longings fulfilled: "There lip to lip and soul to soul they kissed."[50] This is in line with Ken's assertion in "Sion" that

> In bliss when we each other see,
> Love will ecstatic be,
> And though no marriages are there,
> We yet may, like the cherubs, pair.[51]

In "Edmund" especially the level of technical crudity is only too apparent, and nowhere more strikingly than in the description of heroic action by an angel who saves the martyr heroine from rape just in time:

> God heard, and as her vest away they drew,
> His vehicle her angel o'er her threw;
> The radiant robe struck all the pagans blind,
> Like Sodomites, they groped the door to find.[52]

46 "Edmund," Ken, II, 168.
47 "Hymnotheo," Ken, III, 208.
48 *Ibid.*, III, 210.
49 "Edmund," Ken, II, 254.
50 *Ibid.*, II, 294.
51 Ken, IV, 393.
52 "Edmund," Ken, II, 250–1.

Clearly the Devil had little chance of victory with such supersonic weapons in the hands of God. The angel's vehicle is perhaps the principal piece of spiritual machinery employed by Ken. His use of it certainly reveals the impossibility of writing a Metaphysical epic in a scientific age.

CHAPTER SIX

POETIC DICTION

In the final analysis it is not enough to identify Ken's verse as the last written in the Metaphysical tradition. It is also necessary to show that tradition being eaten up by the encroachments of poetic diction, in the form of a specialised and stereotyped devotional vocabulary. An account of these encroachments will suggest that Ken's verse is of no mean historical and critical importance. To detach from his work what is perhaps the leading single strand, the tone and technique directly influenced by Herbert, is to be aware of the sources of poetic diction in the central tradition of Metaphysical devotional poetry. In this strand of Ken's work the trend towards fossilisation is dominant, and we have a picture of the fortunes of the religious lyric from its Elizabethan and Caroline origins to its 18th century redundancy.

Although Ken shows marked symptoms of the decline and decadence of the Metaphysical lyric, he was not cut off from the Elizabethan idiom. He seems, like Herbert, to have had access to the grave simplicity and delicate seriousness of the pre-Metaphysical lyricists. It is difficult in the following passage to put one's finger on any languid decadence which would suggest its having been written in the 1690s rather than in the 1590s:

> Shouldst Thou, thy face awhile to hide,
> Retire to thy celestial bride,
> And while thou dost from me recede,
> On lilies feed,
>
> Thither I after thee will fly,
> And hymning thee, will prostrate lie,
> In hope to pluck a lily sweet,
> Kissed by thy feet.
>
> Odour and Beauty never fade,
> In lilies sweetened by thy shade,

'Twill Virtue from the touch derive,
Love to revive.[1]

There is of course a marked Herbertian tone in the last verse, and in the technical device of the short end-line; but only in the second line of the second stanza is there a clear hint of the avalanche of poetic diction, which, in the bulk of Ken's work, stifles the life of the lyric.

Even in the heroic couplet Ken is able to retain the freshness of tone and purity of diction characteristic of the Elizabethan lyric:

Fixed on its root a lily grows,
Keeps grateful scent and lovely look,
And never falls, tho' rudely shook.[2]

It is indeed remarkable that the same man could write, in the style of an 18th century hymn:

My Jesus, while I thee enjoy,
I'll on thy Love my powers employ.[3]

Nashe and Herbert on the one hand, Watts and Wesley on the other, with Ken bridging the gap; the claim seems extravagant. And yet, when we try to measure the span within Ken's own work, it is this transition, or at least one aspect of it, which is revealed.

What one is forced to recognise at the outset is that Ken could write in the idiom of the Renaissance lyric, even when he was not following the specifically Herbertian strain of devotional verse. He may not excel in this idiom, but he does not always strike the outlandish note which one would expect from someone using the techniques of bombastic hyperbole and Renaissance rhetoric in the 1690s. Even in a pastoral, Ken can indulge in an argumentative conceit:

Fond lovers' deaths no shepherdess should dread,
They'll soon have resurrection from the dead,
The next kind maid whom on the plains you meet
Rekindles all your amorous vital heat.[4]

The pastorals of Norris are tame neoclassical affairs compared to the provocative Metaphysical wit which Ken's juxtaposition of sacred and profane creates. Ken also seems able to indulge in hyperbole:

[1] "Jesus in our Retreat," Ken, I, 436–7. The movement and theme of the last verse recall the last verse of George Herbert's "Virtue."

[2] "On the Blessed Blandina," Ken, IV, 522.

[3] "Jesus Present," Ken, I, 426.

[4] "Damonet and Dorilla," Ken, IV, 514.

I thirst, I thirst, O cool me, for I burn,
My very bones will into cinders turn;
. . . .
Should I suck all the moisture from the flowers,
Or should I drink up all the April showers,
Or bathe myself all o'er in morning dew,
Yet still my thirst my ardours would renew;
. . . .
Should I, like Noah's dove, range all about,
With the vast deluge strive to quench my drought,
And drink the universe of waters dry,
Back to the ark I yet should thirsty fly.[5]

The copious amplification of Renaissance eloquence is not yet spent, and the decadence we might expect is missing from these extracts. Here then is Ken's starting point. Unless these lyrical resources are recognised, any analysis of their rapid wastage would be misleading.

Ken conserved a good measure of his lyrical resources when writing in the vein of Herbert. The collapse into poetic diction is neither immediate nor inevitable. From time to time Ken relieves the grey monotony of his verse with a gentle pun, a touch of introspective quaintness, or a dash of aggressive spirituality. Thus he will not have his mind lost in rhapsody; it must show that it has profited by its exercise:

When thou hast new disoveries made,
At every coast thy spirit lade,
That I a rich return may have.[6]

The conceit was a commonplace. Ken uses it as a cliché. But Ken's pun on "return" – coming back and profit – forestalls the incipient poetic diction. Without this Herbertian twist the verse would be tame.

The same is true of Ken's introspective quaintness, which at times nicely avoids being caught up in the trite machinery of devotional diction. In his "Hymns on the Attributes of God," the Metaphysical techniques taken over from Herbert militate against fossilisation:

My guilty conscience me accused,
That I my love had long misused.
. . . .
'Twas hard my love to disembroil,
'Twould often toward the world recoil.[7]

[5] "Thirst for Jesus," Ken, I, 526–7.
[6] "Christophil," Ken, I, 417.
[7] "Infinity," in "Hymns," Ken, II, 7.

I had some short lived joys in view,
Which I was eager to pursue;
But God's preventing love stept in,
To guard from sin.[8]

We are a long way from Samuel Clarke's demonstrations of the attributes of God; Ken does not allow the abstract attributes to smother the still small voice of conscience, with its taste for intimate self-revelations and quaint self-dramatisation. But the relationship between the attributes of God and the workings of the conscience is a fragile one, and Ken found it easy to fix this relationship in a specialised technical vocabulary, which squeezes the personality of conscience into the well-worn channels of ritual anonymity. Hence the modification into the following style:

Rewards, Attractive, Object, Aid,
Love irresistibly persuade;
Yet Love to raise a gentle awe
Became a Law.[9]

Here the ritualistic diction of the first line severely handicaps the unmistakably Herbertian lyric life; the quaintness and the sweetness are reduced to a mere trickle.

Ken was also capable of the kind of devotional violence which characterises Herbert's verse. In a tone which the 18th century would have considered grossly uncivilised, he could write:

If up to heaven Thou wilt ascend,
Though heaven I cannot open rend,
Though I want wings to soar,
Where seraphs thee adore,
I'll draw thee down from heaven by violent prayer,
To visit me, and re-assume my care.[10]

But more often than not, Ken expresses his aggressive spirituality in a kind of devotional shorthand which dispenses with the techniques of its Metaphysical sources:

My prayers with damps and wanderings are possessed,
Foul impious thoughts me on my knees infest;
My crazy spirit a strange tedium feels,
In that which only my distemper heals.[11]

[8] "Wisdom," *ibid.*, II, 55.
[9] "Psyche," Ken, IV, 260.
[10] "Jesus Present," Ken, I, 427.
[11] "Hymnotheo," Ken, III, 178.

A crazy spirit afflicted with tedium is a subject around which Herbert, and later Hopkins, wove their intricate self-revelations. Ken too creates a sense of spiritual energy thwarted by the doldrums of ennui, but the potential immediacy of his writing is diminished by the poetic diction of "damps" and "wanderings." These abbreviations stand for emotional processes which Herbert and Hopkins were better equipped to trace.

Both Herbert and Hopkins were subject to the encroachments of poetic diction. Their achievement is to have resisted so successfully the stultification of the spirit by the form. Ken gives in to the temptation all too easily. By doing so, he illustrates how the Metaphysical tradition in devotional poetry died out. The techniques which Herbert used to reveal the foibles of the human soul, with its selfishness, its blindness, its slowness, and yet also its charm, modesty and sensitivity, become in Ken's hands at best a means of analysing the mechanics of spiritual discipline, and at worst a way of telling his beads in a strangely lifeless and public manner.

These beads, with their prearranged message, were to become an 18th century idiom, designed to present gnomic religious slogans. Byrom would tell his beads in an attempt to popularise the ideas of Law. Here is one of Ken's gnomic slogans:

> None skill the outgoings, and resorts of wind,
> Much less the spirit's workings on the mind.[12]

This is the way Byrom liked to argue. The 18th century understood the language of propositions; and, in a sense, Ken, by reducing the quaintness, wit and subtlety of the Metaphysical mode to the level of a public proposition argued from analogy, is making available to the 18th century, truths which would otherwise have been rejected as outlandish. He is Metaphysical enough to have a personal Holy Ghost, but the activities of this spirit are sufficiently straightforward not to shock the piety of the Augustans:

> My Holy Chost is prone,
> To comfort me in every moan.[13]

Ken was thus able to retain the Metaphysical idiom in the context of an overall Augustan purpose, at the expense of rigidity of poetic diction.

[12] "Psyche," Ken, IV, 214.
[13] *Ibid.*, IV, 278.

The "outgoings" and "resorts," which are rationalisations of complex Metaphysical moods, crop up again in the "Anodynes":

I sooner could of shifting wind,
The rise, recess and wheelings find,
Than of my heart detect the wiles,
By which it daily me beguiles;
Its strange reserves black guilt to hide,
Lest by repentance it should be descried.[14]

This sounds like a paraphrase of a Herbert poem; there is no movement, simply statement. The argument is a proposition based on analogy, but it is couched as a personal not a general assertion. Relics of Metaphysical intricacy lie about in the isolated single words, which stand for something no longer in the poem. "Rise," "recess," "wheelings," "wiles" and "reserves" sit awkwardly, unrelated to each other or anything else, except the semi-allegorical, semi-conceptual figures of "Guilt" and "Repentance." This is one way in which the Metaphysical tradition died out.

Ken does not often reduce the Metaphysical tradition to the simpler modes of 18th century verse. More often he uses its techniques to analyse the mechanics of spiritual discipline. This is very evident in the "Anodynes," where a Metaphysical tone may be exquisitely captured, but made to serve the purposes of a devotional stereotype. There is the example of the defeat of pain according to tactics that appear to be pre-arranged:

Pain, wheresoe'er you change your seat,
I soon discover your retreat;
When you move to and fro,
I your meanders know;
You cannot march so swift about,
But I can nicely trace you out.

When you an ambuscade project,
I instantly the plot detect;
You can have no reserves,
In membranes or in nerves;
But of the foe, my watchful sense
Gives me minute intelligence.[15]

There is a Metaphysical quaintness here, which renders the extended image palatable, a nice balance, maintained by the conceit, between

[14] Ken, III, 431.
[15] Ken, III, 399–400.

attack and defence; and yet the shadows of poetic diction and incipient decadence lie across the life of the poem. Ken seems to be pushing a genuine Metaphysical tone into a pattern so fixed, that it must lead to preciosity and vain repetition. His insistence on the religious significance of pain provides material in which preciosity and poetic diction are seen to be closely linked.

Ken falls into preciosity because he analyses his spiritual life in too mechanical a way. And yet, in so doing, he does not altogether lose the charm of the Herbertian idiom. The relic of a Metaphysical structure sustains an element of wit, and prevents the atrocious lapse of taste into which many an 18th century devotional poet fell. In other words, Ken can be precious without being languid or effete:

> The thought that I should Love immense offend,
> Began my heart to chide, grieve, soften, rend;
> Love shining in, gave with one beam a stroke,
> My heart it into numerous atoms broke;
> And in a tear each atom melting lay,
> As of past outrages I took survey.[16]

The Metaphysical correspondence between "tear" and "atom,"and the way in which "outrages" gathers up and melts down the poetic diction of the first lines, redeems this passage from decadence. The preciosity ceases to be gratuitous by being related to the simple reality of penitential tears.

A similar process can be traced in a parallel passage where once again the relic of a Metaphysical structure checks the incipient decadence of the melting mood:

> For my sins past, soft tears I shed,
> And as each tear fell from my head,
> Out of my joints a needle came,
> I by degrees transpired my flame;
> And soon as I had all my sins deplored,
> I sweet vacation gained from being gored.[17]

Here the preciosity depends on the correspondence between tears and needles, and further, between tears, needles and sins. The mechanics are crude, but the tone of "sweet vacation" is unmistakably Herbertian.

When Ken is at his liveliest his Metaphysical heritage survives the encroachments of poetic diction. Sometimes however his decadence

16 "God is Love," in "Hymns," Ken, II, 110.
17 "Anodynes," Ken, III, 441.

is the result of theme and attitude rather than style and technique. Take for example the crude masochism of:

Let Love immense his work fulfil,
My pains instructive cure my will;
Love saw me cool, I by his rod
Shall re-enamoured be of God.[18]

the traditional preciosity of:

Her womb not long could God enfold,
I'll fast my God for ever hold.[19]

or the languid tone of the phrase "most agreeably tired."[20] These specimens reveal a built-in decadence at the level of content, and this aggravates the structural inadequacies of Ken's work.

One of the ways in which Ken allowed poetic diction to encroach on the Metaphysical tradition was by his willingness to use doctrinal rather than devotional material when it suited his purposes. The life of the spirit is broken down into its operative parts, like a piece of clockwork. It is as if Ken was doing for the spirit what men accused Hobbes of having done with the soul or mind.[21] Certainly when he writes devotional verse based on doctrinal spare parts, the supposed conflict he presents is artificial and lifeless. Hopkins and Herbert struggled with their God, but their struggle was a human one, not a mechanical one. Ken can be surprisingly lifeless and hollow:

Long I with God for mastery had tried,
Antarctic wills in me for empire vied;
My rational alone to heaven inclined,
My sensual with the world and Satan joined;
God, grace, heaven, reason, conscience, inward peace,
All strove, me from my tyrant to release;
Lapsed nature, the vain world, and powers of hell,
And sensual pleasures moved me to rebel.[22]

[18] *Ibid.*, III, 417.
[19] "Sion," Ken, IV, 412.
[20] "Unity," in "Hymns," Ken, II, 36.
[21] One of Hobbes's admirers, John Glanvill (1664–1735), eulogises him in terms which are also applicable to Ken's poetic diction:

"In pieces took here we are shown the whole
Clockwork and mechanism of the soul;
May see the movements, labyrinths and strings,
Its wires and wheels and balances and springs."

Quoted in Fairchild, I, 19.
[22] "Resignation of Jesus," Ken, I, 501.

This marshalling of abstracts has only nominally to do with the spiritual life. It is not even a contribution to polemical discussion in the way of the following antithetical definition of sin and right reason:

> Sin with by-rills devaricates the stream,
> And raises idols to our fond esteem;
> But when right reason has the channel freed,
> To disembogue in God we flow with speed.[23]

In like manner, Ken treats the resurrection along doctrinal rather than devotional lines. Using a conceit, which the Metaphysicals applied directly to the resurrection of the dead, Ken writes in argumentative analogy:

> Should every drop in vapour rise,
> Turn rain, hail, snow, when in the skies,
> Thence falling into earth be sunk,
> And up by vegetables be drunk,
> God all their shiftings can compute,
> And into dew them retransmute.[24]

The implicit faith of the Metaphysicals is giving way to the propositional argument from analogy, so dear to the 18th century. Ken cultivates this doctrinal tone:

> Our birth propension sensual sows
> To wilful sin, which cherished grows;
> We all our life must God invoke,
> That growth to choke.[25]

This is the gnomic tone and pietistic argument that Byrom, in the 18th century, so often employed in defence of the spirit and the religious life.

In the final analysis, Ken does not so much retail an evaporated Metaphysical tradition to the needs of the 18th century, as fossilise this tradition in the poetic diction of mechanical devotion. In a rare reference to the technique to which he was attached, Ken wrote:

> Ejaculations are pearls loose;
> Strung, Meditation they produce.
> 'Tis by continuation, Thought
> Is up to Contemplation wrought.[26]

[23] "Hymnotheo," Ken, III, 242–3.
[24] "Resurrection," Ken, IV, 46.
[25] "Psyche," Ken, IV, 213.
[26] "Meditation on Jesus," Ken, I, 430.

Unfortunately, in poetic terms, the pearls are too often loose, and too rarely strung. The result is the following:

> My Jesus now my spirit fills,
> His love in suavities distils,
> Preventions, tractions sweet,
> Devout Christ-hymning heat;
> Kind checks, and calls benign, and gracious might,
> And coruscations of the joys in light.[27]

The specialised vocabulary is a characteristic of Ken's devotional verse. Later on we find "coldnesses and damps,"[28] "calls, checks, waitings,"[29] "interruptions, damp and cold";[30] and of angels we are told:

> They feel no tedium, damp or chill,
> God totally exhausts their will.[31]

This poetic diction, which encrusts Ken's lyricism, was an end-product of the Metaphysical tradition.

Ken's attempt to perpetuate the tradition was in itself laudable. It was doomed to failure because he was himself too much a part of that tradition in a derivative sense. The conjuncture in which he wrote, together with the slightness of his individual talent, determined that it could not be otherwise. It was left to the radically new classicism of the early 18th century to evolve in the hymn a successful poetic diction for devotional verse. Ken, apart from being interesting as a poet who kept alive (or was kept alive by) the Metaphysical tradition as late as the 1690s, is, by virtue of the variety of his styles and techniques, a figure who illustrates quite clearly the various possibilities and redundancies available to the religious lyricist at the turn of the century.

[27] "Jesus Present," Ken, I, 425.
[28] "Desire," Ken, I, 524.
[29] "God's Grace," in "Hymns," Ken, II, 108.
[30] "God is Love," *ibid.*, II, 111.
[31] "Psyche," Ken, IV, 312.

PART TWO

JOHN BYROM AND WILLIAM LAW

CHAPTER SEVEN

LIGHT AND ENLIGHTENMENT

At the most conscious level Byrom and Law followed the political and religious tradition of Sancroft and Ken; they were high-church Tories. Byrom, as a man of the world and a layman, formally accepted the Hanoverian establishment, though he had strong Jacobite tendencies. Law, like Ken before him, was more scrupulous, and at the moment of crisis, in his case 1715, became a non-juror. They thus belonged to the fringes of the consensus without being totally excluded from the pale. Fortunately they were not exclusive brethren and did not deliberately separate themselves from the central milieu of debate.

If one considers that the tradition of Sancroft and Ken had dwindled into the eccentricity of non-juring Jacobites setting up the so-called British Catholic Church, then Byrom and Law must be seen as transcending the limitations of their impoverished heritage. In the first place their contacts with the new religious ferment which challenged the establishment provide a link between 17th century and 18th century dissent, at the very moment when Defoe and Watts were succeeding in associating the traditional forces of dissent with the new régime. And in the second place Byrom and Law register and participate in the controversy at the heart of the English Enlightenment. Byrom was particularly good at registering; it was usually Law who laid down and initiated the lines of participation.

Byrom's rôle is nonetheless crucial. His contacts with the various tendencies in English thought were remarkably catholic for a man nourished in a dwindling and extremist tradition. Although he was for a time a disciple of Malebranche, he also had access to the high-priest of Enlightenment metaphysics, Samuel Clarke:

I went in the morning to pay a visit to the famous Dr Clarke of St James's ... Mr Glover is a great disciple of his, and knowing me a disciple of F.

Malebranche, ... was very well pleased to hear the confabulation, which you may be sure was mighty philosophical.[1]

One may suspect that controversy brought down to an Addisonian level of coffee-house confabulation may lack the rigorous method and intellectual integrity of the old-style polemic. But Byrom's tactics surely suited his age. For all his amateurish bonhomie, his persistence in taking sides in confabulations of this sort ensured that what Locke would have called "obscure enthusiasm" had its say in the genial parrying of 18th century coffee-house dilettantes.

Byrom fulfilled his rôle of registering the intellectual trends of his age with casual but insistent eclecticism. The opinions he collects and expresses are on the whole grouped around the confrontation between the upholders of Light and the upholders of Enlightenment.[2] The Clarke/Malebranche confabulation is exemplary in this respect. Byrom does not always register these two trends as opposites, but the distinction is always there. Three examples from the years 1735–1737 will illustrate how casual and insistent Byrom's eclecticism is, and how succinctly if superficially he registers the intellectual development of his day.

In 1735 we find him preoccupied on the same day with Norris and Pope. His interlocutor

talked much of Mr Norris, said that God spoke to all his creatures within themselves – ... that the ideas of all things were in God, and that we existed in him from all eternity; ... talked about Mr Pope and gave him a good character, and his *Essay on Man*; we read Norris, some parts, his letter about his niece's death, his contemplation of man's end, his 139th Psalm.[3]

In 1736 we find him flitting from one coffee-house to another, from fascination with the strangeness of a resuscitated medieval mystic to fascination with the daring opinions of a modern deist:

Went to North's coffee-house... Saw Josiah there, who had met with Walter Hilton, old edition... Thence to Richard's... Mr Reynolds the Deist there; talked with me strangely, and I should not talk and hear such things.[4]

[1] J. Byrom to Mrs Byrom, 4 January 1728, *Remains*, I, 287.

[2] This distinction is made by Rosalie Colie in *Light and Enlightenment: A Study of the Cambridge Platonists and the Dutch Arminians* (Cambridge: University Press, 1957).

[3] Diary, 20 June 1735, *Remains*, I, 632.

[4] Diary, 15 March 1736, *ibid.*, II, 15. Walter Hilton (d. 1396), a monk, wrote *The Scale of Perfection* which appeared in printed editions in 1494 and 1506, after which it remained unpublished until 1869. Hilton's other works include *A Devoute Boke* (printed in 1516) and *A Devoute Treatyse* (printed in 1521). *DNB*

In 1737 Malebranche, Norris and Walter Hilton are joined by a spokesman for the very latest mystical movement, namely Zinzendorf's Moravianism. In this entry Byrom appears to be registering, perhaps unwittingly, the beginnings of a way out of the Clarke/Malebranche antithesis. The Enlightenment is present in the form of the ubiquitous deist, Mr Reynolds, "who told me to read *The Moral Philosopher*."[5] After several comings and goings, "Mr Watley came in and talked about some Zinzendorf, a primitive Christian."[6] In between these brief appearances on the part of latter-day apostles of Light and Enlightenment, there is a cryptic reference to "the gentleman that had changed his classical taste for mystical."[7] This third man, who is not named, had merely ordered a book by a 16th century Portuguese mystic. This entry nevertheless marks a turning-point; the second half of Byrom's journal is full of references to the new mystical trends in English religious life, and it is no accident that he sees them replacing an established classicism. By the 1740s, classicism and the Enlightenment were being seriously undermined by the forces of preromanticism and evangelicalism, and the Clarke/Malebranche confrontation was no longer an issue.[8]

It is against this framework of casual registering of vast trends that the impact of Law on Byrom must be seen. From Law, Byrom drew a solid cause and committed insights which qualify his eclecticism and give some coherence to his otherwise random contacts. The structure of Law's thought depended on his interpretation of Jacob Boehme. From the German mystic Law felt he could derive a scientifically based ideology. To support his interpretation of Boehme, he claimed that Sir Isaac Newton had been "a diligent reader of that wonderful author," and had derived from him his "three first properties of eternal Nature."[9] Byrom faithfully reported that, according to Law,

[5] Diary, 31 March 1737, *Remains*, II, 101. The first volume of Thomas Morgan's *Moral Philosopher* was published in 1737. Morgan was a self-styled "Christian Deist," who did "little more than reflect the arguments of Tindal and Toland." See Leslie Stephen, *History of English Thought in the 18th Century*, I, 73, 140.

[6] Diary, 31 March 1737, *Remains*, II, 102. Ludwig von Zinzendorf (1700–60) was a leader of the Moravian pietists.

[7] *Ibid.*, II, 101.

[8] Cf. Fairchild, I, 208–9 on the links between evangelicalism and preromanticism. The Countess of Huntingdon not only financed her own evangelical sect, but also distributed her patronage to Thomson, Shenstone and Savage.

[9] William Law, *Some Animadversions* (1740), in *Works*, ed. G. B. Morgan (9 vols.; Brockenhurst and Canterbury: privately printed for G. Moreton, 1892–3), VI, 201. On the influence Boehme may have had on Newton, and on Law's interpretation of this influence, see S. H. Hobhouse, *Selected Mystical Writings of William Law. With Studies in the Mystical Theology of William Law and Jacob Boehme, and An Inquiry into the Influence of Jacob Boehme on Isaac Newton* (2nd ed. revised; London: Rockliff, 1948), pp. 397–422.

Sir Isaac Newton ... had shut himself up with one Dr Newton for three months in order to search for the Philosopher's Stone from Jacob Behmen, that his attraction and the three first laws of motion were from Behmen, that Behmen best explained himself, that in short all was over as it were, all laid open.[10]

Law may have appreciated Newton's debt to Boehme, but, as Byrom's closing phrase cryptically reveals, he considered that Newton had gravely misapplied Boehme's philosophy. Law is really concerned to reinstate Boehme as a living light whose glory has been obscured by the pseudo-science of a dead Enlightenment.

In two places Law clarifies his criticism of Newton's treatment of Boehme, and develops his own interpretation, or, as he would have it, lets Boehme explain himself. In *The Spirit of Love* (1752–4) Law corrects Newton and presents the cornerstone of his own philosophy:

Here also, that is, in these three properties of the desire, you see the ground and reason of the three great laws of matter and motion lately discovered, and so much celebrated; and need no more to be told, that the illustrious Sir Isaac ploughed with Behmen's heifer when he brought forth the discovery of them. In the mathematical system of this great philosopher these three properties ... are only treated of as facts and appearances, whose ground is not pretended to be known. But in our Behmen, the illuminated instrument of God, their birth and power in eternity are opened... Not a particle of matter stirs, rises, or falls, separates from, or unites with any other, but under their power. Not a thought of the mind, either of love or hatred, of joy or trouble, of envy or wrath, of pride and covetousness, can rise in the spirit of any creature, but as these properties act and stir in it.[11]

By laying open Boehme in this way, Law is forging a philosophical instrument by which to distinguish life and death as well as truth and error. Philosophy for Newton meant natural philosophy; for Law it means moral philosophy.

In *The Way to Divine Knowledge* (1752) Law makes a definitive and formal statement of this argument which Byrom had recorded nine years earlier. He refers to the previous age (c. 1661–2) when Boehme first came to the attention of the Royal Society:

When he first appeared in English, many persons of this nation, of the greatest wit and abilities, became his readers; who, instead of entering into his one, only design, which was their own regeneration from an earthly to an heavenly life, turned chemists, and set up furnaces to regenerate metals, in search of the Philosopher's Stone.[12]

[10] Diary, 30 May 1743, *Remains*, II, 364.
[11] Law, VIII, 19.
[12] Law, VI, 196.

The core of Law's philosophy can be identified in these two passages. The central argument that he derives from Boehme and passes on to Byrom is that living light involves the inner man, and that all else is alchemy.

This, in the final analysis, is the light to which Byrom and Law bear witness. It opposes in almost every respect the Enlightenment which conditioned the prevailing religious consciousness of the early 18th century. We catch an interesting glimpse of the characteristics of this heterodox light in the following extracts:

> *Byrom*: Went to the Devil Tavern to enquire for any of my acquaintance, but none there; dined there alone upon a mackerel... Thoughts after dinner. Is there not in all or most words an inward and an outward meaning? The body! and the shadow! When truth rises in the mind at first it makes a long shadow, but when it is vertical, and shines perpendicularly through us, little or no shadow... The substance and the form.[13]

> *Law*: In the regions where light is sprung up, whence superstition is fled, where all that is outward in religion seems to be pruned, dressed and put in its true order, there a cleansed shell, a whited sepulchre, seems too generally to cover a dead Christianity.[14]

Byrom has his metaphysical moments brought on by a lone meal of mackerel, and Law is in the middle of a vast treatise designed to prick the minds of all that doubt; but both describe in visual imagery the categorical distinction between inner light and outward Enlightenment.

[13] Diary, 5 June 1729, *Remains*, I, 366–7.
[14] *Appeal to All that Doubt* (1740), Law, VI, 282.

CHAPTER EIGHT

DEISM AND MODERNISM

The stand made by Byrom and Law is no isolated rearguard action; it arises directly out of the prolonged religious controversy of the early 18th century. Some analysis of this controversy is necessary if we are to make sense of Byrom's subsequent propaganda for Law's new way of ideas, and his expression of their latent aesthetic consequences. It will be sufficient to describe Byrom's contacts with the two leading schools in this controversy, on the one hand the deists, on the other the modernist defenders of orthodoxy.[1]

Bishop Butler is traditionally regarded as the arbiter in this debate; his was the last meaningful word and his the modest victory over the reluctant heretics. Butler however was no giant-killer, and the deists were more like paper tigers than dragons. In a sense, the deist controversy only becomes meaningful when it is viewed from a distance, through the eyes of Byrom and Law at one end, and through the eyes of Mandeville at the other.

From diametrically opposed positions, Byrom and Mandeville arrive at a similar diagnosis of the intellectual and spiritual poverty of the deist/modernist debate. By daring to apply reason to the heart of the matter, they follow the line of argument laid down by Swift in *An Argument against Abolishing Christianity*. Like Swift they start with the categorical distinction between real and nominal Christianity. Thus Byrom in 1729 is echoed by Mandeville in 1732:

Byrom: I find the young folks of my acquaintance think Mr Law an impracticable, strange, whimsical writer, but I am not convinced by their reasons... But for Mr Law, and Christian religion, and such things, they are mightily out of fashion at present; indeed I do not wonder at it, for it is a plain, calm business, and here people are, or love to be, all of a hurry,

[1] For a readable and judicious critical account of this controversy, see Leslie Stephen's *History of English Thought in the 18th Century* (1876).

and to talk their philosophy, their vain philosophy, in which they agree with one another in nothing but rejecting many received opinions; their arguments all centre chiefly in this, that Christianity being now established, another kind of conduct is proper from that which might be required at its first appearance; to which I answer, that indeed they have established a nominal Christianity and forsaken the practical Christianity, that – but I cannot talk of Christianity in a coffee-house.[2]

Mandeville: Among those who outwardly show the greatest zeal for religion and the gospel, I see hardly any who teach us, either by precept or example, the severity of manners which Christianity requires. They seem to be much more solicitous about the name, than they are about the thing itself.[3]

It is a sign of the times that the polemicists of the deist controversy dismissed Mandeville as the ghost of Hobbes, and Byrom and Law as newfangled enthusiasts; the nominal Enlightenment was thus depriving itself of the real lights available to it.

The significance of the stand made by Byrom and Law can be measured when set in the context of the long reign of Locke over 18th century thought. Locke was used by both sides in the deist controversy, with the result that his contribution to the Enlightenment, though pervasive, was emasculated. Byrom and Law belong to the few outside the French Enlightenment who felt the full force of Locke's philosophy.

Byrom owed this insight in the first instance to the reactionary nature of his family background. He was warned about Locke while still at the university, his father communicating to him his own splendid prejudice:

I have not Mr Locke's book of Human Understanding, it is above my capacity; nor was I ever fond of that author, he being (though a very learned man) a Socinian or an atheist, as to which controversy, I desire you not to trouble yourself with it in your younger studies. I look upon it as a snare of the devil, thrown among sharp wits and ingenuous youths to oppose their reason to revelation, and because they cannot apprehend reason, to make them sceptics, and so entice them to read other books than the Bible and the comments upon it.[4]

Byrom's father was not alone in his apprehensions as to the effect of

[2] J. Byrom to Phebe Byrom, 18 February 1729, *Remains*, I, 328–9. Cf. Byrom's report of Law's remark that a certain Dr Cheyne "was always talking in coffeehouses about naked faith, pure love." Diary, 30 May 1743, *ibid.*, II, 363.

[3] Bernard de Mandeville, *A Letter to Dion*, ed. J. Viner ("Augustan Reprint Society," No. 41; Los Angeles: University of California Press, 1953), p. 63.

[4] Edward Byrom to John Byrom, 16 September 1709, *Remains*, I, 7.

Locke's philosophy upon university students. In 1702 Henry Lee published his *Anti-Scepticism*, a page by page refutation of Locke's *Essay Concerning Human Understanding* (1690). Byrom, up at the university in 1709, may well have seen Lee's book, the preface of which was addressed "To the author's two sons in the universities." In this preface Lee spelt out in no uncertain terms the materialist and atheist implications of Locke's philosophy.

Lee's two most telling points run as follows. In the first place, Locke is a materialist:

> This word Reflexion is all new, for in common language it can signify nothing else but Knowing or Consciousness: and it seems a little uncouth, to make Knowing or Consciousness a source or fountain of knowledge. Besides if it be true which this author plainly insinuates, ... that 'tis as probable that our souls are matter indued with the faculty of thinking, as immaterial substances, then what he calls Reflexion may be only doubled motion, or, in Mr Hobbes's language, Re-action, and so we have only that new name of Reflexion for motion modified by an organised body, to keep up the handsome port of a distinction between material and immaterial substances and their operations; whereas really and in plain English they are just the same.[5]

In the second place, Locke is an atheist:

> For if there be no laws of nature, but such as we must learn from experience and conversation, then no sort of action can be a breach of them, but what is disagreeable to a man's own present judgment and opinion, ... and at that rate moral goodness, which is the glory and excellency of the divinity itself, will become mutable, precarious and only nominal.[6]

Lee's views are both anachronistic and prophetic; for while they look back to Cudworth's already doomed attempt to defend the immutability of the soul and morality, they also look forward, albeit with terror, to the enthusiastic materialism and atheism of Holbach, La Mettrie and Sade.

Byrom no doubt learnt from Lee as well as from his father about this insidious aspect of the Enlightenment. He was thus prepared from an early age for Law's later onslaught against the school of Locke. In Law's trenchant words, written in 1751,

> to be trained up in the school of reason, and to have learnt from Locke or Le Clerc, and such like masters, how to be reasonable Christians, is to be

[5] Henry Lee, *Anti-Scepticism: or Notes upon each chapter of Locke's Essay* (London, 1702), Preface.

[6] *Ibid.*

taught how to be content with eating dust and serpent's food instead of the tree of life.[7]

The English Enlightenment, however, shied away from this vision of Locke, and it was left to a French philosopher of German extraction, Holbach, to point the moral from the vantage point of 1770:

Comment le profond Locke ... et comment tous ceux qui, comme lui, ont reconnu l'absurdité du système des idées innées, n'en ont-ils point tiré les conséquences immédiates et nécessaires? Comment n'ont-ils pas vu que leur principe sapait les fondements de cette théologie qui n'occupe jamais les hommes que d'objets inaccessibles aux sens, et dont par conséquent il leur était impossible de se faire des idées?[8]

Byrom and Law, like Holbach, recognised the full force of Locke's philosophy. They were consequently able to see through the tame sterilities of the deist controversy.

Byrom's attitude to the religious controversy of his day can be deduced from his remarks on the men and books of note that he came across. The frame of reference is as wide as the controversy itself, though Byrom's comments are fragmentary and peremptory. Certain figures, such as Woolston and Warburton, come in for special attention, but in the last resort deists and modernists are classed as kindred spirits.

Byrom came across the latest books by Toland, Collins, Tindal and Pope among the deists. The entries on Toland and Collins were written in the years 1725–6, before Byrom had become a disciple of Law, and reveal his eclectic curiosity.[9] Tindal and Pope on the other hand, in entries made in the 1730s, after Byrom had espoused the cause of Law, are put in their place, albeit cryptically in the case of Tindal and tentatively in the case of Pope.[10]

A similar trend can be traced in Byrom's personal contact with deists. In 1725 a group of freemasons upstairs excites his curiosity,[11] and in February 1729, only a few days before his momentous meeting with Law, he notes without further comment that "the Deist club

[7] Law, Letter to William Briggs, March 1751, printed in J. H. Overton, *William Law Nonjuror and Mystic* (London: Longmans, 1881), p. 347.

[8] Holbach, *Système de la nature* (1770), quoted in Henri Talon, *William Law. A Study in Literary Craftsmanship* (London: Rockliff, 1948), p. 9.

[9] *Remains*, I, 109, 186, 223.

[10] "Mr Prior ... was within, but seemed to look wild, I thought, mightily, and he was reading *Christianity as Old as the Creation*, I was concerned at his looking so strangely." Diary, 15 June 1735, ibid., I, 628. "Mr Balls ... brought Pope's *Essay* for me to read, and I found fault." Diary ,July 1736, *ibid.*, II, 55.

[11] Diary, 20 April 1725, *ibid.*, I, 121.

met at the Golden Lion in Fleet-street on Thursdays (I think), and at the Bull's Head in Ludgate-hill every Sunday."[12] The turning point is registered in June 1729. On the day before the famous mackerel dinner he had a long discussion with two deists, Pits and Strut:

> We had much talk; Pits a true Deist; Strut said he did not believe a future state; I told him I was more concerned for him than for any man in bedlam... Strut talked about personal identity; that a man was not the same person for two moments; that it was consciousness, according to Locke.[13]

Byrom did not need Holbach to tell him that deism and atheism relied heavily on Locke's epistemology. When Pits and Strut accost Byrom two years later for further discussion, Byrom, reinforced by Law, participates in an attempt to get Strut at least to "embrace Christianity."[14]

Byrom may have enjoyed his encounters with Pits and Strut, but in later life he came to see that the controversy between deist and divine was sterile. Orthodox or heterodox, they were fighting each other in the same boat:

> So deist and divine, but both in vain
> Seek to unfasten the prophetic chain![15]

This slogan of 1750 is expanded into treatise form in Law's *The Way to Divine Knowledge* (1752).

Law's summary of a generation of religious controversy deserves more attention than it has received. He writes with measured impatience of twenty years spent in "this dust of debate":

> I had frequently a consciousness that the debate was equally vain on both sides, doing no more real good to the one than to the other, not being able to imagine that a set of scholastic, logical opinions about History, Facts, Doctrines, and Institutions of the Church, or a set of logical objections against them, were of any significancy towards making the soul of man either an eternal angel of heaven, or an eternal devil of hell.[16]

The tone and structure of the argument remind one of Gibbon, a laconic surface controlling the underlying passion, the heat of rhetoric

[12] Diary, 4 February 1729, *ibid.*, I, 323.
[13] Diary, 4 June 1729, *ibid.*, I, 366. It was this discussion which gave rise to Byrom's mackerel-dinner mediation; he appears to have felt the force of the argument for free-thinking.
[14] Diary, 3 January 1731, *ibid.*, I, 445.
[15] "On Middleton Concerning Prophecy," lines 867–8, *Poems*, II, 239.
[16] Law, VI, 153.

running in clear, cool channels. Law goes on to spell out his conclusion:

I would not attempt to show from Reason and Antiquity, the necessity and reasonableness of a Divine Revelation in general, or of the Mosaic and Christian in particular. Nor enlarge upon the arguments for the credibility of the Gospel History, the reasonableness of its creeds, institutions and usages; or the duty of man to receive things above, but not contrary to, his reason. I would avoid all this because it is a wandering from the true point in question, and only helping the Deist to oppose the Gospel with a show of argument, which he must necessarily want, was the Gospel left to stand upon its own bottom.[17]

For Law, the giant that Bishop Butler was supposed to have slain was no giant but a cardboard scarecrow. It follows that

the learning of the Christian world must bear the blame of these fruitless disputes: the demonstrators of the truth and reasonableness of Christianity have betrayed their own cause, and left true Christianity unmentioned in their defences of it. What a Reasonableness of Christianity have some great names helped us to?[18]

For Law, deism is a mere by-product of theological decadence:

Deism has no natural foundation, or ground of its own, to stand upon; it does not grow from any root or strength within itself, but is what it is merely from the bad state of Christendom, and the miserable use that heathenish learning and worldly policy have made of the Gospel.[19]

There is a good deal of truth in this; English deism was parasitic. It faded away with the soggy orthodoxy that nourished it. With the rise of evangelicalism, English deism revealed its incapacity to stand on its own feet, and, unlike its French counterpart, it failed to develop into a full-blooded and fruitful atheism.

The French atheists would no doubt have agreed with Law's analysis of English deism. As it happens, in England, Mandeville's views on this question coincide with Law's. In his *Letter to Dion*, he makes an analogy between the profession of Christianity and the profession of Freemasonry. Freemasons, he claims,

pretend to mysteries, and eat and drink together; they make use of several ceremonies which are peculiar to themselves, with great gravity; and with all this bustle they make, I could never learn yet, that they had anything to do, but to be Free-Masons, speak well of the honour of their society, and

[17] Law, VI, 150.
[18] Law, VI, 159.
[19] Law, VI, 177.

either pity or despise all those who are not members of it. Out of their assemblies, they live and converse like other men. And though I have been in company with several of them, I profess, unless I am told it, I can never know, who is a Free-Mason, and who is not.[20]

Both Law and Mandeville seek to overtake the inanities of a hollow controversy between deist and divine, and restate the problem in terms of the name and the thing.

Byrom's contacts were not exclusively with the deist side of the controversy; he was from an early age familiar with the physico-theological school of modernists. In the same academic year that he warned his son to beware of Locke, Byrom's father commended to him Ray's *Wisdom of God in the Creation.*[21] Later on Byrom kept up with the second generation of physico-theological apologists. He seems to have got more out of the questionably orthodox Wollaston, than from Derham's staid vulgarisations of the Newtonian scheme of things.

His diary for 1725 contains four entries on Wollaston and only one on Derham.[22] This may have been partly because he confused Wollaston with Woolston; and Byrom considered Woolston to be a well-meaning if fitful enthusiast, caught up in a controversy the ground of which he did not accept. Still, even if Byrom was aware of Wollaston's identity, there is some reason for his preferring him to Derham, for Wollaston's *The Religion of Nature Delineated* was written with a modicum of rationalism, virtue being deduced from truth, to the distaste of the orthodox physico-theological school who, in their flight from the 17th century art of reasoning, preferred to deduce it from a sense of innate benevolence.[23]

In spite of his lack of enthusiasm for Derham, Byrom kept himself informed of the latest goings-on at the Royal Society, and followed the dispute between Clarke and Leibniz on the force of bodies.[24] And he

[20] Mandeville, p. 64.

[21] Edward Byrom to John Byrom, 5 April 1710, *Remains*, I, 12.

[22] *Ibid.*, I, 95–130 (Wollaston); *ibid.*, I, 181 (Derham). William Derham (1657–1735), FRS (1702), contributed to the Royal Society Transactions from 1697 to 1729. His Boyle Lectures of 1711–12 were published as *Physico-Theology* (1713) which ran to twelve editions by 1754. This was followed up by *Astro-Theology* (1715) which reached a ninth edition in 1750, and *Christo-Theology* (1730). His popularity continued unabated until he was superseded by Paley. *DNB*

[23] William Wollaston (1660–1724) followed Samuel Clarke's lead in developing his intellectual theory of morality. His book was privately printed in 1722. The first public edition (1724) sold ten thousand copies within a few years. His orthodoxy was questioned and he was occasionally confounded with the far more heterodox Thomas Woolston who was at the same college. *DNB*

[24] Diary, 29 February, 1728, *Remains*, I, 295.

records the views of another leading member of the Royal Society, Desaguliers, who was prepared to reduce metaphysics to the state of natural logic.[25] In the long run however Byrom takes but brief notice of the arguments of the physico-theological school. He is more eloquent when he writes of Woolston and Warburton, and more effective when he writes of Butler and Stillingfleet; but he deals with these particular modernists after his 1729 meeting with law.

Thomas Woolston is one of the rare figures in the deist controversy who comes to life and has some human interest. Byrom seems to have felt this, though it is not until 1729 that he involves himself with Woolston. The 1725 entries on Woolston are as non-committal as those on Wollaston.[26] Up to the beginning of 1729 Byrom merely talks about Woolston's books:

> Shrove Tuesday, boiled lamb and steaks and pancakes and fritters; talk of Woolston's sixth book just come out, which Glover said was the worst of all; smoked a pipe.[27]

This was the sixth of Woolston's *Discourses on the Miracles*, the first having appeared in 1727. By this time Woolston was very much a public figure, having caused a scandal in 1725 with *A Moderator between an Infidel and an Apostate*, in which he carried his allegorical interpretation of scripture to the point of questioning the historicity of the resurrection and virgin birth.[28] In November 1725 the government indicted him for blasphemy, and it was only through the efforts of the considerably more heterodox yet more worldly-wise Whiston that the prosecution was called off.[29] The government however resumed prosecution after the publication of the fourth discourse in 1728, and Woolston was tried by the Lord Chief Justice on the 4th of March 1729, and found guilty on four counts. He was sentenced to a year's imprisonment and a fine of one hundred pounds; unable to

[25] Diary, 1 July 1729, *ibid.*, I, 383. John Theophilus Desaguliers (1683–1744), son of a Huguenot refugee, Freemason, FRS (1714), author of *A Course of Mechanical and Experimental Philosophy* (1724), inventor of the planetarium and the ventilator, is said to have been the first man to deliver learned lectures to general audiences. *DNB*

[26] "We clubbed 6d. apiece to buy Woolston's *Moderator*." "I went to my chamber and wrote some out of Woolston." etc. Diary, 22 March to 25 May 1725, *Remains*, I, 99–143.

[27] Diary, 18 February 1729, *ibid.*, I, 328.

[28] Woolston adopted his idea of interpreting scripture allegorically from Origen. *DNB*

[29] William Whiston (1667–1752), divine and Boyle lecturer (1707), was accused of Arianism in 1710 and deprived of his professorship. Author of *Primitive Christianity Revived* (1711) and *Athanasius Convicted of Forgery* (1712), he started up a society for promoting primitive Christianity which was attended by Baptists, Unitarians and Deists, and to which Clarke and Hoadly were invited. In 1747 he joined the Baptists. *DNB*

pay the fine, he remained in custody until his death in 1733 at the age of 63.

A fortnight before the trial, and only a day after his Shrove Tuesday talk with Glover, Byrom paid Woolston a visit. He depicts Woolston as a well-meaning enthusiast floundering in the inhospitable waters of the deist controversy:

Thence to Woolston's, where I went up to him and bought his sixth book, and sat with him half an hour; he said he could not drink half a pint of wine but it put him out of order, that he went to bed early and rose when it was light; that he had no relations or friends in the world; that he had no notice of his trial, which was to be according to the papers on Saturday; that it was reported that he kept a club of Deists, but it was not true; that he never conversed with Collins, nor would not do if he should ask him; that if the clergy would let him alone he would let them alone; . . . that he was but thirty years old when he began to think of this allegorical way; . . . that he had done with pulpiting. I made several objections to him, but he seemed to shuffle them off by a spiritual Christ that was in us, and we in him, and he in God, which could not be the man Christ; in short I could not tell what to make of him.[30]

In the weeks preceding Woolston's trial, Byrom struggled to answer this peculiarly sympathetic brand of spiritualism,[31] and a year later he returns to this subject with an entry of poignant brevity: "talked of Woolston, I cried out against all persecution."[32] Long after Woolston's death, Byrom notes that he has been reproached for defending Woolston and being "a professed unbeliever."[33]

Woolston was a lone figure, whose insights corresponded to a certain extent with those of Law and Byrom. He had indeed begun to think in his allegorical way at the turn of the century, and had published his findings in 1705.[34] His method led him to bouts of enthusiasm which were frowned on by both sides in the deist controversy. Thus he had published in 1720 *A Letter upon this question: Whether Quakers do not the nearest resemble the primitive Christians*, as a result of which he was deprived of his fellowship; and in his *Third Freegift to the Clergy* (1723), he talks of being "carried up in vision" and having "an interview with Elias."[35] Byrom and Law took a great interest in the

[30] Diary, 19 February 1729, *Remains*, I, 329–30.

[31] "We talked about the world having a beginning, which he thought it had, that Woolston was wrong to write against the established religion as he did." "Thought of answering Woolston's book, sat writing shorthand in answer to Woolston's book till past two o'clock." Diary, 26 February and 1 March 1729, *ibid.*, 333, 336.

[32] Diary, 1 February 1730, *ibid.*, I, 421.

[33] Diary, 19 February 1739, *ibid.*, II, 238.

[34] Thomas Woolston, *The Old Apology for Christian Religion Revived.*

[35] *DNB*

phenomenon of 18th century Quakerism; and while they would clearly condemn Woolston's oscillation between vague and irresponsible enthusiasm on the one hand, and frequent compromise with the conventions of modernist apologetics on the other, they could appreciate Woolston's tendency to ignore the evidence of the letter, and shift the ground of the controversy to the evidence of the spirit.

And yet in the final analysis, Byrom and Law recognised that Woolston belonged to the modernist school. The *Six Discourses on the Miracles* were if anything in advance of the 18th century modernist movement.[36] Byrom and Law on the other hand argued along lines which render redundant the whole range of modernist apologetics. The ground they choose to defend is not that of evidences, but of the basic distinction between real and nominal Christianity, that ground in fact which, as Mandeville pointed out, was outside the preoccupations of the deist controversy:

> Once it is taken for granted, that to be a Christian, it is sufficient to acquiesce in being called so, and attend the outward worship of some sect or other, it saves the clergy a vast deal of trouble, from friends as well as foes. For to quiet and satisfy all scrupulous consciences, is as great a drudgery as it is to write in defence of miracles.[37]

And still the modernists went on drudging; thus 1727 saw the publication not only of Woolston's first discourse, but also of Warburton's *Inquiry into the Causes of Prodigies and Miracles.*

If Byrom and Law looked on Woolston with sympathetic curiosity, they regarded Warburton with considerable hostility. For where Woolston wrote as often as not in his allegorical way, Warburton was the champion of literal evidence, and in his *Divine Legation of Moses* (1738) proffered a weighty reprimand to the demythologising tendencies of Woolston. Byrom's distaste for Warburton's literalism appears in his *Epistle to a Gentleman of the Temple* (1749), where, following his "master Law," he exclaims:

> "Life," "death," and such-like words, in scripture found,
> Have certainly an higher, deeper ground,
> Than that of this poor perishable ball,
> Whereon men doat as if it were their all –
> As if they were like Warburtonian Jews,
> Or Christians named, but still no higher views.[38]

36 "The vigour of the 'Discourses' is undeniable, and it has been said with some truth that they anticipate the mythical theory of Strauss." *DNB*

37 Mandeville, p. 63.

38 Lines 431–6, *Poems,* II, 164.

The correspondence of 1751–2 between Warburton and Byrom reveals their diametrically opposed positions.

Warburton, with characteristic frankness, describes these positions as follows: "You would convince men of the truth of the Gospel by inward feelings; I, by outward facts and evidence."[39] The formula is fair, but, in a letter to Hurd, Warburton spelled out the implied corollary with similar downrightness. Byrom is ipso facto a raving enthusiast:

> He is certainly a man of genius, plunged deep into the rankest fanaticism... He is very libellous upon me; but I forgive him heartily, for he is not malevolent, but mad.[40]

The correspondence continues with Warburton suggesting that Byrom confine his enthusiasm to poetry,[41] and Byrom defending himself and Law with considerable brio:

> Though I am neither Hutchinsonian, Methodist, nor monk, yet, where you charge them in the lump with dulness, madness or misanthropy, you seem to do it with a vivacity as free from argument as it is from malice... I will confess to you that what most affected me was a note that treated Mr Law's *Appeal* as a system of rank Spinozism (which passes commonly, you know, for Atheism), by one who has defended Mr Pope from that atrocious imputation, so compendiously, that in one page of the *Appeal* (p. 302) the sum of all the arguments in favour of the poet appear in the divine's discussion of Dr Trapp's unthinkingness about enthusiasm; and one has the satisfaction to see in one particular (the want of which in others, respect to great abilities forces an enthusiast to regret – and vigorously) Law and Warburton agreed. Can you will that I should wish it to be, or enjoy it while it is so in the main – Warburton and Trapp?[42]

Byrom's parenthetic rhetoric and elliptical syntax provide a cover of

39 W. Warburton to John Byrom, 12 December 1751, *Remains*, II, 523.

40 Warburton to Hurd, 3 January 1752, quoted in *Poems*, II, 177–8.

41 "As to enthusiasm it is generally agreed that there are two sorts, an innocent and a hurtful. The first of which is chiefly employed in drawing pictures from the imagination, the other in advancing opinions as the result of the judgment ... In the places you refer to in my writings, where I speak of enthusiasm, it is plainly of the harmless kind, a warm and vigorous effort of the mind, exerted on subjects of the imagination ... I think the literary world loses by your not applying your talents more to poetry, in which you appear naturally formed to excel." W. Warburton to J. Byrom, 3 April 1752, *Remains*, II, 533–4. It will be seen from this extract that Warburton's Augustanism, at once neoclassical and latitudinarian, is impeccably orthodox.

42 J. Byrom to W. Warburton, 10 April 1752, *ibid.*, II, 537–8. Joseph Trapp (1679–1747), first Professor of Poetry at Oxford (1708–18) and high-church Tory, assisted Sacheverell at his trial (1709–10) and enjoyed the patronage of Bolingbroke. One of his four discourses on the "nature, folly, sin and danger of being righteous overmuch" (1739) was preached against, and in the presence of, George Whitefield. One anonymous reply to Trapp was entitled *Dr Trapp Vindicated from the Imputation of being a Christian*, to which he replied with *The True Spirit of the Methodists and their Allies* (1740). *DNB*

polite compliment and sweet reasonableness to his indictment of Warburton. By referring to Warburton's defence of Pope, Byrom insinuates the lesser charge of inconsistency, but the last phrase rings out the basic antagonism. The opposites are polarised around Law and Trapp; Warburton belongs to the camp of Trapp.

Byrom rarely rose to such range and compression of argument, and once the confrontation with Warburton was over he relied on formulae and catch-phrases to castigate his bête noire. Thus in subsequent poems he coins the word "bibliolatry" to characterise Warburton's literalism. To the Warburtonians who "think that now religion's sole defence / Is learning, history and critic sense,"[43] Byrom exclaims: "'Tis perfect Bibliolatry to me."[44] The exponents of bibliolatry rely on the letter and make the spirit dependent on the letter; Byrom mimics the Warburtonian position:

> To look for inspiration is absurd;
> The Spirit's aid is in the written Word:
> They who pretend to his immediate call,
> From Pope to Quaker are fanatics all.[45]

Byrom distinguishes between "the men of Spirit and the men of Books."[46] Of the men of books, he notes ironically:

> Such is the text before us, and so plain
> The Saviour's promise which the words contain,
> That men, for modern erudition's sake
> Must read and study to acquire mistake.[47]

And in a more frontal attack, several years later, he returns to this favourite theme:

> "The Comforter," Christ said, "will come again,
> Abide with, dwell in" – not your books, but – "you".
> Just as absurd an ink-and-paper throne
> For God's abode, as one of wood and stone!

43 "Familiar Epistles to a Friend upon a Sermon by Rev. Mr Warburton" (c.1752), Letter III, lines 15–16, *Poems*, II, 258.

44 Ibid., II, 260 (line 62). If the date of 1752 is correct, then this is the first recorded use of the word "bibliolatry," antedating by eight years the instance (see Note 48 below) in "A Stricture on the Bishop of Gloucester's Doctrine of Grace" (c.1760), to which both Skeat and the *OED* give priority. See W. W. Skeat, *An Etymological Dictionary of the English Language* (Oxford: Clarendon Press, 1910).

45 *Poems*, II, 259 (Letter III, lines 25–8).

46 *Ibid.*, II, 267 (Letter V, lines 27–8).

47 *Ibid.*, II, 262 (Letter IV, lines 7–10).

If to adore an image be idolatry,
To deify a book is bibliolatry.[48]

Byrom's strictures on Warburton's defence of Christianity reveal the crux of the distinction between Light and the Enlightenment. It is no accident that they take the form of a critique of the letter by the spirit, a critique which had been initiated by the Cambridge Platonists a hundred years previously.

Byrom's strictures on Warburtonian literalism obviously owe much to Law's own contribution to this controversy. Law published his *Short but Sufficient Confutation of the Rev. Dr Warburton's Projected Defence of Christianity* in 1757. In this pamphlet, Law lays out the basic elements from which a critique of the letter by the spirit can be built. It is evident that he has Swift and Berkeley behind him. Swift had mercilessly devastated those abuses which arose from a reliance on either the spirit or the letter; from the neutral, transparent and yet positive ground of common sense, he played one extreme off against the other, reducing both the language of the spirit and the spirit of learning to the crude nonentity of wind.[49]

Berkeley is on somewhat less transparently neutral ground when he uses Swift's technique to defend the free spirit against the encroaching literalism of the minute philosophers. His Alciphron takes an Aeolist position, and is prepared to demonstrate the mechanical operation of the spirit, but Berkeley, through the words of Euphranor, turns Alciphron's critique of the spirit into a critique of the letter:

Alciphron: O Euphranor! He who looks into the bottom of things, and resolves them into their first principles, is not easily amused with words. The word *inspiration* sounds indeed big, but let us, if you please, take an original view of the thing signified by it. To *inspire* is a word borrowed from the latin, and strictly taken, means no more than to breathe or blow in; nothing therefore can be inspired but what can be blown or breathed; and nothing can be so but wind or vapour, which indeed may fill or puff up men with fanatical and hypochondriacal ravings...
Euphranor: ... To *discourse* is a word of latin derivation, which originally signifies to run about; and a man cannot run about but he must change

[48] "A stricture on the Bishop of Gloucester's Doctrine of Grace" (c. 1760), *ibid.*, II, 278. According to Skeat and the *OED* this is the first recorded instance of the word "bibliolatry" (but see Note 44 above).

[49] See in particular the Aeolists' theory in *A Tale of a Tub*: "Words are but wind; and learning is nothing but words; ergo, learning is nothing but wind." Swift, I, 97. Cf. *The Mechanical Operation of the Spirit*: "For, it is to be understood, that in the language of the spirit, cant and droning supply the place of sense and reason, in the language of men." Swift, I, 182.

place and move his legs; so long therefore as you sit on this bench, you cannot be said to discourse.[50]

Law, who like Berkeley is defending the free spirit against the slavery of literalism, takes his stand on considerably less neutral ground.

Law indeed proffers an eccentric and partisan theory of ideal language in an attempt to illuminate "the shining sons of verbal literature, whether critics, linguists or grammatical orators."[51] To all such practitioners who are concerned with the mechanical operation of language, Law proclaims his own organic theory:

The language of every creature is natural, and not taught; it is as much the effect of its whole nature, the joint operation of its soul, spirit and body, as its life is; and is articulate, or not articulate, good or evil, harmonious or horrible, just as the life of the creature has more or less of the perfection of a divine, or earthly harmony in it.[52]

From this mystical and unassailable position, Law launches out at Warburton with characteristic energy:

The doctor has by strength of genius, and great industry, amassed together no small heap of learned discussions of points, doctrines, as well heathenish, as Christian, much the greatest part of which, the Christian reader will find himself obliged to drive out of his thoughts, as soon as he can in right, good earnest say with the jailor, "What must I do to be saved?" This collection of decisions he calls his projected defence of Christianity, which if it was such, Christianity must have been but poorly provided for its support by the four gospels. I shall make no doubt of his intending, what he says, by them. But a *Project* in defence of Christianity, is not more promising, than a *Trap* to catch humility. The nature of things allows no more of the one, than of the other. To be a defender of Christianity, is to be a defender of Christ, but none can defend him, in any other sense, or degree, than so far as he is his follower.[53]

Law brings to his critique of Warburtonian literalism some of the insights of Berkeley, and some of the ironic clarity of Swift, but his positive purpose is perhaps nearer to the Cambridge Platonists' defence of the free spirit than to Swift and Berkeley's passionate concern for the via media of common sense. The following thrust at Warburton conveys the essential flavour of Law's style and stance:

If it could be supposed, that any man was a hundred times more knowing than the doctor is, in what he calls his enigmatic, curiologic, hieroglyphic, emblematic, symbolic, etc., etc., profundities, yet if all the beasts of the

[50] Berkeley, p. 237.
[51] *Short Confutation of Warburton*, Law, VIII, 211.
[52] *Ibid.*
[53] *Ibid.*, VIII, 211–12. Note the pun on Trap(p).

field, and all the fowls of the air, were to be brought before him to be distinguished from one another, by articulate sounds of his voice, even such a man would be as unequal to the task, as a Tom Thumb.[54]

Both Law and Byrom thus contributed to the critique of the letter by the spirit in an age when literalism was a hall-mark of deists and modernists alike.

In 1737 Byrom discussed Christianity with two latitudinarian heroes, Butler and Stillingfleet. Byrom's record of these two conversations speaks as eloquently of the nature and tone of modernist apologetics as any of the polemical exchanges between Law and his latitudinarian opponents. The evening of Byrom's encounter with Bishop Butler was in March; Butler stayed with him for two hours before supper:

I mentioned the saying, "Credo quia impossibile est," and Dr Butler told of that saying of Tertullian, and I contended for the justness of that expression, that it was that where reason was not a proper judge, it being a thing impossible to reason, where faith was to believe; that man had a heart capable of being faithful as well as a head capable of being rational, and that religion applied itself to the heart. The Dr talked with much mildness and myself with too much impetuosity... Dr Butler stayed about or above two hours, till about eleven o'clock, and went away, and we supped, and I ate some bread and cheese and drank a glass or two of sack, and said I wished I had Dr Butler's temper and calmness, yet not quite, because I thought he was a little too little vigorous.[55]

The quaint way in which Byrom does justice to the mildness of Butler's temperament, while wishing it less mild, reveals the wide divergence between their views as to the respective merits of heart and head in religion.

The conversation with Benjamin Stillingfleet, grandson of the pioneering latitudinarian bishop, took place a month later:

Fell a-talking about Christianity, and Stillingfleet said that the morality exemplified by the Gospel was of much greater consequence than the doctrine of the Incarnation, the Trinity etc., and that a man might be as good a Christian without believing them; to which I said, that if it was the doctrine of Christians, I did not see how he could be called so good a Christian that did not believe it; and he seemed to be warm upon that head, and to ask who were good Christians? ... and he had much ado to distinguish Mahometans from Christians without the doctrine of the Trinity, as indeed he might well.[56]

[54] *Ibid.*, VIII, 210.
[55] Diary, 28 March 1737, *Remains*, II, 97, 99.
[56] Diary, 20 April 1737 *ibid.*, II, 119. Benjamin Stillingfleet (1702–71) was something

Byrom feels that Stillingfleet, by insisting on morality above doctrine, is sapping the roots of Christianity. Byrom prefers to distinguish between the name and the thing, and thus avoids Stillingfleet's difficulty. At the level of nominal religion there is indeed no difference between the Christian, with or without the Trinity, and the Mahometan. As Mandeville never tired of saying,

> all men who are born of Christian parents, and brought up among Christians, are always deemed to be such themselves, whilst they acquiesce in, and not disown the name: but unless people are palpably influenced by their religion, in their actions and behaviour, there is no greater advantage in being a Christian, than there is in being a Mahometan or a Heathen.[57]

In the same year, Dr Hartley pointed out, in a letter to Byrom, that nominal religion is one thing and real Christianity another:

> I should be sincerely glad to hear what good and wise men say in regard to the doctrine of the Trinity; but I had rather see one man reclaimed from a bad life by being made to accept Christ for his lord and master, and by imitating his example, than a hundred men be made converts either to Dr Waterland or Dr Clarke.[58]

Byrom no doubt heartily concurred with these sentiments. He was not greatly impressed with either Butler or Stillingfleet. His dialogue with them merely serves to increase his sense of their irrelevance to the main question.

Byrom's opposition to the luke-warm apologetics of the modernists is succinctly summed up in his pastiche of Addison's hymn, "The spacious firmament on high." In it he writes, possibly as early as 1725:

> What though no objects strike upon the sight, –
> Thy sacred presence is an inward light.
> What though no sounds should penetrate the ear, –
> To listening thought the voice of truth is clear.
> Sincere devotion needs no outward shrine:
> The centre of an humble soul is thine.[59]

The substitution of "inward light" for "reason's ear" and of "an humble soul" for "the spacious firmament," is of the essence of Byrom and Law's critique of the religious consciousness of the English Enlightenment.

of a dilettante and possibly the original "blue-stocking" (he actually wore blue stockings when frequenting the salons of Bath). In the 1740s he became a follower of Hutcheson and in the 1750s a disciple of Linnaeus. *DNB*

57 Mandeville, p. 62.

58 Dr Hartley to J. Byrom, 6 September 1737, *Remains*, II, 187. David Hartley (1705–57), the founder of Associationism, was on friendly terms with Butler and Warburton as well as with Byrom and Law. He was widely read in the early Fathers and his rationalism does not preclude a tendency to strong religious feeling. *DNB*

59 "A Penitential Soliloquy," *Poems*, II, 53–4.

CHAPTER NINE

FROM QUIETISM TO EVANGELICALISM

Before considering in more detail the structure of thought to which Byrom and Law were committed, we must take note of the sources and influences which in large measure determine its nature, and certainly modify its tone and colour. As may be expected it is in Byrom that these sources and influences can be traced, standing alongside and in stark contrast to his contacts with the deist controversy. Law rarely mentions his sources and influences outside the central one of Boehme; and though on more than one occasion he poured cold water on Byrom's eclectic and obscure enthusiasms, these were more often than not enthusiasms he shared, while wishing to purge them of their eccentricities and excesses.

The sources and influences unearthed by Byrom in his search for kindred spirits, with whom he could join in common cause against deists and modernists alike, can be divided into two separate groups. The first group comprises men and books of the distant and not so distant past, ranging from medieval mystics to the quietists of the previous generation, and including some notice of contemporary Quakerism. The second group covers Byrom's contacts with the new Moravian and Methodist movements.

Byrom's contacts with the first group were primarily through books, and though he had discovered Malebranche and Antoinette Bourignon before his meeting with Law, it is noticeably after 1729 that he manifests a growing interest in the mystical and quietist traditions. He seems to have amassed a collection of books which one would not have supposed to be in circulation in the second quarter of the 18th century. Thus at an auction in 1731, he bought

Thomas à Kempis' works, ... Savonarola's *Life*, ... Malebranche's *Morality*, ... Van Helmont's *Great and Little World*, ... *Ignatius Loyola*

Essercitii Spir... In another shop I bought Pordage and *Philothea* of ... John of the Cross.[1]

A week later he "bought some books, among the rest two pieces of Jacob Behmen."[2] Byrom came to Boehme through Law. From Boehme he moved to Johannes Tauler, a 14th century German mystic, whom he paraphrases in "The Beggar and the Divine."[3] He also paid some attention to the late Renaissance idealists and alchemists, Van Helmont, Pordage, and Thomas Vaughan alias Eugenius Philalethes; this last was supposed by some to be still alive in 1735.[4] And from the Catholic mystics, St John of the Cross and Thomas à Kempis, Byrom moved back to the age of Tauler and beyond in search of men and women who had written about divine love. Among the treasures he unearthed were long-forgotten works by Walter Hilton,[5] Margery Kempe,[6] and Duns Scotus.[7]

In large measure Byrom was following his own will-o'-the-wisp curiosity in this research, and Law himself would have approved of few of the writers he unearthed. For Law, even Boehme had to be read with rigorous caution, and one can imagine what a diatribe he would have pronounced against the gothic antics of Van Helmont or Thomas Vaughan, when one recalls his opinion of their much less gothic contemporary Henry More, whose philosophy he qualified as Babylonian rant, babble and gibberish.[8] Byrom on the other hand, undismayed, left it to his friend to control his eclectic enthusiasms, and went his own sweet way, talking about witches over tea as late as 1739.[9]

[1] Diary, 13 January 1731, *Remains*, I, 447. Franciscus Mercurius van Helmont (1618–99) developed out of Paracelsus a kind of monadology which foreshadows the theories of Leibniz. His father J. B. van Helmont (1577–1644) was one of the first followers of Paracelsus. *Diccionario de Filosofia.* John Pordage (1607–81), astrologer and mystic, described by Baxter as the chief of the Behmenists, established a community to seek the highest spiritual state through visible communion with the angels. Accused of pantheism (1651) and witchcraft (1654), he instructed Jane Lead in the principles of Behmenism from 1663 and was the author of *Theologia Mystica* (1683). *DNB*

[2] Diary, 20 January 1731, *Remains*, I, 452.

[3] *Poems*, II, 387.

[4] Diary, 2 May 1735, *Remains*, I, 601. Thomas Vaughan (1622–66), author of *Magia Adamica* (1650), was killed by fumes of mercury while pursuing his alchemical researches. *DNB*

[5] Diary, 13 January 1735, *Remains*, I, 551–2.

[6] Diary, 19 June 1735, *ibid.*, I, 631. Margery Kempe's late 14th century autobiography remained unpublished until 1936.

[7] Diary, 25 March 1736, *ibid.*, II, 22.

[8] See below, p. 110.

[9] Diary, 19 February 1739, *ibid.*, II, 235–8. At this tea-party a Mr Stonehouse said "that he did not doubt but a great part, the greatest I think, of his congregation, were such as would have communion with the devils that night, that the air was full of devils ..."

But if Byrom often let his curiosity get the better of his judgment, it is important to notice that, before he embraced the cause of Law, he had found a significantly coherent master in Malebranche.

A cult of Malebranche appears to have developed among the second generation of non-jurors who organised themselves as such after the 1715 Hanoverian settlement. Byrom was in close touch with the non-jurors and Jacobites of Manchester, and he shared his enthusiasm for Malebranche with his friend Dr Deacon. Thomas Deacon had been ordained in the non-juring succession by Jeremy Collier, and professed so high an Anglicanism that he found his spiritual home in the newly formed British Catholic Church.[10] Another kindred spirit was Alexander Forbes, a Jacobite mystic, much influenced by the tradition of French quietism.[11] To these men Fénelon and Malebranche were modern saints who upheld the light of spirituality in an age of ersatz Enlightenment.

In 1727 Byrom acquired an image of his saint, a portrait of Malebranche.[12] He wrote a poem of Browningesque gusto on this purchase.[13] Dr Deacon responded to his friend's enthusiasm in a letter which reflects Byrom's own feeling towards Malebranche:

You see I am in a rambling way, and who knows but in time I may be a little like your worship? for I have been reading Malebranche this last week. When Mrs Byrom sent me Bekker, she sent with him the first vol. of Malebranche's *Metaphysics* and the second of his *Morality*; broken pieces as they are, I have read them. You will easily imagine where I was, when his *Metaphysics* was the first book I ever read of his – I was lost, absent, up in the clouds, sunk into nothing, absorbed in l'infini, not in company with myself, but with la raison universelle, la sagesse éternelle, la vérité in-

[10] Thomas Deacon (1697–1753) was ordained by Jeremy Collier in 1716 and became a non-juring bishop in 1733. A founder-member of the "True British Catholic Church" in Manchester, he was active in the 1715 Jacobite rebellion. Three of his sons joined the Pretender in 1745 and one of them was executed. Jeremy Collier (1650–1726), author of *A Brief Essay Concerning the Independency of Church Power* (1692) as well as the celebrated *Short View of the Immorality and Profaneness of the English Stage* (1698), became a non-juring bishop in 1713 and, following the death of Hickes (1715) the leader of the non-jurors. *DNB*

[11] Alexander Forbes (1678–1762) came under the influence of Fénelon and Mme Guion while in France, took part in both Jacobite rebellions, and published *Essays Moral and Philosophical* (1734). *DNB*. It is interesting to note that among the non-jurors gathered around Dr Deacon was John Clayton (1709–73), a friend of the Wesleys. Through Clayton, Wesley found his way as a preacher into the non-juring congregations of Manchester.

[12] *Remains*, I, 237.

[13] "On Buying the Picture of Father Malebranche" (1727). Byrom's tone and syntax remind one of Browning: "Not a word whose it was; but, in short, 'twas a head," "Done at Paris .../In the year ninety-eight, – sixty just from the birth/Of the greatest divine that e'er lived upon earth." *Poems*, I, 82, 84.

térieure, l'ordre immuable; in short I own myself ravished with him... I am resolved to read all his works carefully in order.[14]

Both Byrom and Dr Deacon seem to be taking an infectious delight in something rather out of the way, something at variance with the spirit of the age.

Byrom in particular obviously derived great pleasure from using Malebranche as his champion in argument. Thus in 1729, after his meeting with Law, he persists in his good-humoured hero-worship of Malebranche:

Very merry about F. Malebranche, Shakespeare.[15]

Much talk with Dr Green about the old dispute of Cartes, F. Malebranche, seeing all things in God, where else? ... He laughed much, all very merry; I defended Malebranche as saying the same as Paul, "In him we live and move," etc., self-evident truths, the idea of God the best proof of what really had none, that the light within was the true scheme if rightly understood.[16]

This is a far cry from Norris's weighty paraphrase of Malebranche's speculative philosophy. It does however help to explain the persistent appeal of Cudworth, the champion of "la raison universelle" and "l'ordre immuable," of whom Byrom himself wrote, in a poem on "The True Grounds of Eternal and Immutable Rectitude": "Cudworth perceived."[17] Furthermore, it makes sense of Law's unique attempt to link "la raison universelle" with "la vérité intérieure," an attempt made, not out of the blue, but in the context of this particular tradition.

Byrom went on talking about Malebranche, even when Law was beginning to take over as his mentor; there was no break in his discipleship, and in 1730 Dr Deacon identifies the common cause of the two leaders as the defence of real Christianity:

Thomas à Cattell ... believes Mr Law may be a good man, but his book does harm with weak judgments, and Father Malebranche is a visionary, etc. O Christianity, where art thou to be found? Not amongst the clergy.[18]

Byrom was also aware that Norris represented the Malebranchian

[14] Dr Deacon to J. Byrom, 14 May 1727, *Remains*, I, 252. Balthasar Bekker (1634–98) was a Dutch Cartesian and author of *De Betooverde weereld* (The World Bewitched, 1691–3). *Enciclopedia Filosofica.*

[15] Diary, 16 December 1729, *Remains*, I, 392.

[16] Diary, 31 December 1729, *ibid.*, I, 399.

[17] *Poems*, II, 412.

[18] Dr Deacon to J. Byrom, 20 February 1730, *Remains*, I, 429.

tradition in England,[19] and in his only reference to Berkeley, he notes: "Berkeley a man of genius, but a little whimsical. Berkeley's system approaches something to Malebranche's."[20] By this time (1737) he is convinced that whimsy is out of place, that he himself had perhaps been over-whimsical in his attitude to Malebranche, and that Law is the only source of truth unsullied by whimsy. And yet he does not ignore those whom he would consider to be Law's precursors, and Ken at least is a name he reveres.[21]

There is one further major enthusiasm of Byrom's, previous to his contact with Law, which has passed unnoticed. It needs to be mentioned because it calls attention to the phenomenon of extreme quietism, and because it gave rise to severe strictures by Law who thereby sought to impose an intellectual discipline on a flabby and amorphous tradition. We refer to the influence of Antoinette Bourignon (1616–1680).[22]

Byrom's enthusiasm for Mlle Bourignon seems to have replaced his enthusiasm for Malebranche. In the same year that Dr Deacon is, on Byrom's recommendation, digging into the works of Malebranche, Byrom himself is beginning to turn his attention to Mlle Bourignon.[23]

[19] "One of my twopenny books is Mr Norris's *Father's Advice to his Children*, wherein I found the commendation of Father Malebranche's book." Diary ,17 June 1729, *ibid.*, I, 377.

[20] Diary, 15 April 1737, *ibid.*, II, 107.

[21] Byrom wrote a 128-line poem in praise of Ken, entitled "A Letter to a Lady, Occasioned by her Desiring the Author to Revise and Polish the Poems of Bishop Ken." *Poems*, II, 114–26. He also possessed four editions of Ken's *Practice of Divine Love*, at the end of one of which he wrote down some quotations from Boehme. See *Poems*, II, 416.

[22] Antoinette Bourignon set up an orphanage and religious cloister in Lille in 1658. She was tried for witchcraft in 1662. From 1663–7 in Malines she developed her antagonism to Rome and gained her first important disciple, Christian de Cort. From 1667–71 in Amsterdam she developed her antagonism to all churches, including Anabaptists, Mennonites, Moravian Brethren, Quakers and Labadists. In 1671 she set up her own community on the island of Nordstrand; persecution, including confiscation of her printing press, mob violence and assassination attempts, followed until the collapse of the community in 1677. Impeached by the Lutheran magistrates for founding a new sect, she sought refuge in the castle of Baron Dodo of Knyphausen at Lutzburg. Unfortunately the Baron was susceptible to visions and accused Mlle Bourignon of witchcraft with power to enlarge and contract her person. She died the same year, a refugee from every kind of existing society. See A. R. Macewen, *Antoinette Bourignon, Quietist* (London: Hodder and Stoughton, 1910), pp. 37 ff. Mlle Bourignon's quietism was characterised by a violent indictment of the word by the spirit. Thus she wrote: "I read no more, because God taught me inwardly all that I needed." Macewen, p. 34. Justification by faith, she declared, was "an idea which stinks in God's nostrils. To promulgate it is to sin against the Holy Ghost." *Ibid.*, p. 69. Her verse is at least as erotic as Mme Guion's; e.g.:

"Mon Jésus, ma douce flamme!
Cessez de me caresser:
C'est trop à mort me blesser,
De votre amour qui m'enflamme!
Ah, mon Jésus doux,
Qu'il est beau de mourir pour vous!" *Ibid.*, p. 37.

[23] "We talked much about Antoinette Bourignon as we went along." Diary, 22 December, 1727, *Remains*, I, 283.

Three years later he notes that a friend has come across the collected works of Mlle Bourignon,[24] and, in a letter to another friend, he confesses: "I grow so passionately in love with her that there may be need to check me a little."[25] About the same time he composed a little poem in Latin celebrating his heroine,[26] and translated two of her lyrics for inclusion in the Wesleys' *Hymns and Sacred Songs* (1739).[27] As a consequence Byrom acquired a reputation as a Bourignonist, and came to the attention of the Scottish Bourignonists. In a letter to a third party in 1733, the nephew of the founder of the Scottish Bourignonists writes:

> I am glad you have found so good conversation as Mr Byrom's. Few people in England are better acquainted with the gentlemen that are admirers of the mystic divinity than I am. My father and uncle . . . were vastly fond of it. My uncle was the author of the *Apology for Mrs Bourignon*. I have all her books, to the number I think of 20 volumes, in French.[28]

Thus Byrom is associated with a recrudescence of Bourignonism, a generation after the original controversy.[29]

Byrom's main contribution to the controversy was his poem "Leslie v. Bourignon."[30] He seems to have been particularly concerned to dissociate himself from the opinions of the non-juring Jacobite polemicist, Charles Leslie, whose *Snake in the Grass* lumped Mlle Bourignon with the Quakers. Leslie's purpose was comprehensive and abusive, to defend the interests of the non-juring priesthood at all costs against contamination with the manifold heresies of quietism:

[24] Diary, 19 January 1731, *ibid.*, I, 449–50.

[25] Letter to J. Stansfield, September 1731, *Chetham Library MS*, quoted in *Poems*, II, 559. This is perhaps Byrom's Augustan conscience speaking. By the 1730s Antoinette Bourignon had become a byword for an extremist position which the orthodox via media would not tolerate. See Walter Harte's *Essay on Satire* (1730) where two extremes are scathingly characterised as "fierce Enthusiasts, or Socinians sad,/Collins the soft or Bourignon the mad." Chalmers, XVI, 352. Walter Harte (1709–74) made an eccentric but symptomatic escape from the Augustan via media in later years. Thus, after suffering a stroke in 1766, he wrote *The Ascetic: or Thomas à Kempis: A Vision* (1767), praised Thomas Aquinas as "one of the clearest and purest writers of his time," and based his fable, *The Courtier and the Prince* on the 20th epistle of Antoinette Bourignon's *Traité sur la pieté solide*. See Fairchild, II, 61–3.

[26] "Laudes Antoniettae," *Poems*, II, 558–61.

[27] "A Hymn to Jesus" and "A Farewell to the World," *ibid.*, II, 74–9.

[28] J. Garden to Rev. Mr Hoole, 31 March 1733, *Remains*, I, 519–20. George Garden (1649–1733), an Episcopalian divine in Aberdeen, whose *Apology for Mrs Bourignon* appeared in 1699, was deposed in 1701 for teaching the "damnable errors" of Mlle Bourignon. See *DNB* and Macewen, pp. 8–10.

[29] The 1709 Assembly of the Church of Scotland noted that "dangerous errors of Bourignonism do abound in some places of this nation." From 1711 to 1889 ordinands were required to disown "Bourignian" doctrines. See Macewen, pp. 14–19.

[30] *Poems*, II, 65–8.

> The great design of the Devil is, and always has been, to beat down the priesthood and outward ordinances; knowing that religion must needs fall with them, and men be left senseless and open, to steer without compass, guided only by the winds of enthusiasm. In this cause he has armed the Atheists and Deists to join with the more plausible Enthusiasts and Latitudinarians. These all cry out upon priestcraft.[31]

Byrom's espousal of the cause of Bourignon was no doubt seen by the purist followers of Leslie as an attempt to sink the distinctive separatism of the non-juring tradition into the amorphous movement of contemporary quietism. For quietism had reared its head in England as well as on the continent, and in opting for Bourignon Byrom was committing himself to a recognisable succession of "plausible enthusiasts" who shared a common hostility towards "priestcraft."

In 1697, the year of the second edition of Leslie's *Snake in the Grass*, the Philadelphian Society was founded by Francis Lee, on the basis of the writings of its prophetess, Mrs Jane Lead, whose spiritual diary, *A Fountain of Gardens*, came out in four volumes between 1697 and 1701.[32] Lee's preface to the first volume lays the ground of the quietist stand in terms which would obviously appeal to Byrom and Law:

> I think I can say that I am more than morally assured, that the all-wise God hath hereby ends to bring about, which the most acute and vulturous eye of the greatest Rationalist shall never be able to dive into: and that all will serve but to a fuller breaking out of the truth, and the divine light; that true light, which enlightens every one that comes into the world, so far as it is not resisted, and according to the degree of purity in the vessel, for the reception and reflexion of its rays.
>
> This is an age that thinks itself to excel all that have ever went before it, in the discovery and improvement of truths: and it cannot be denied, but that of these late years Mechanical Knowledge hath been brought up to a very great height, which hath had both its good and bad effects in the world. But notwithstanding all the fancied or real light, in matters either physical or theological; which the present age doth so much boast of; it may perhaps not unfitly enough be said of those that make the chiefest cry, that the veil is still before their eyes.[33]

[31] Charles Leslie, *The Snake in the Grass: or Satan Transformed into an Angel of Light* (3rd ed.; London: C. Brome, 1698), "A Preface concerning Enthusiasm, wherein a short account of Mrs Bourignon," pp. xi–xii.

[32] Jane Lead (1623–1704) studied Boehme under Pordage and experienced almost nightly prophetic visions which she began to write down in 1670. Her other works include *The Heavenly Cloud* (1681) and *The Revelation of Revelations* (1683). Francis Lee (1661–1719) refused the oaths in 1689 and in 1694 became a disciple of Mrs Lead, marrying her daughter by divine order. He was the chief contributor to the *Theosophical Transactions* (1697) of the Philadelphian Society. He composed commentaries on Boehme, edited Thomas à Kempis (1715) and was a pioneer in the foundation of charity schools. *DNB*

[33] Jane Lead, *A Fountain of Gardens*, ed. F. Lee (4 vols.; London: 1697–1701), I, Editor to the Reader.

The consciousness of the incompatibility of Light and Enlightenment is very clearly expressed. Enlightenment is equated with the refined modern age of scientific progress and theological literalism, Light with the one thing needful, divine illumination.

Mrs Lead describes her light in terms which remind us of Cambridge Platonism on the one hand and Byrom and Law on the other. Thus, like the Cambridge Platonists, she opposes intellectual light to the images of sense:

> Wisdom and understanding doth stream forth intellectually, which is the growing nutriment, as it doth pass radically into the soul, as the blood doth into the veins. Now here is a cessation of sensible images, for all is turned into an intellectual sight.[34]

And like Byrom and Law, she opposes the Light of the spirit to the Enlightenment of the letter:

> It is the morning watch and day break of the Spirit, that is to spread forth its light and glory, whereby is to be enlightened the dark ignorant state of the world, who have sat in the region of traditional and literal knowledge, according to the rational wisdom of man, which through the inundation of the Spirit must all be drowned, and a New Earth prepared, wherein the sowing of the Spirit is to be with one pure golden grain, that can admit of no mingling, of what is from man.[35]

It is thus not surprising that Quakerism and quietism were identified in the minds of men like Leslie. For Law, who set himself the task of steering a course between Leslie's die-hard institutionalism and Byrom's naive enthusiasm for Mlle Bourignon, there was the formidable complexity of disentangling the valid insights of Quakers and quietists from their dross and eccentricities. It is worth recording Law's approach to this problem.

In the first place Law entertained doubts as to the ability of either Quakerism or quietism to provide religious panaceas in his day and age. Byrom reports in the year 1737:

> Mr Law . . . talked about Madame Guyon and her forty books, though she talked of the power of quiet and silence, which he believed was a good thing; that indeed it was all, if one had it, but that a person that was to reform the world could not be a great writer, that the persons who were to reform the world had not appeared yet, that it would be reformed to be sure; that the writers against Quakerism were not proper persons, for they

[34] *Ibid.*, I, 8.
[35] *Ibid.*, I, 4–5.

writ against the spirit in effect and gave the Quakers an advantage; that the Quakers were a subtle, worldly minded people, that they began with contempt of learning, riches etc., but now were a politic, worldly society, and strange people.[36]

In the second place Law dissociated the genuine Behmenist tradition from the aberrations of ephemeral organisations such as the Philadelphians:

In the beginning of this century, a number of persons, many of them of great piety, formed themselves into a kind of society, by the name of Philadelphians. They were great readers, and well versed in the language of Jacob Behmen, and used to make eloquent discourses of the mystery in their meetings. Their only thirst was after *visions*, *openings*, and *revelations*. And yet nowhere could they see their distemper so fully described, the causes it proceeded from, and the fatal consequences of it, as by J.B.[37]

And in the third place, in his extremely qualified appreciation of Henry More, Law issued a warning against those who sullied the tradition of spirituality with the dross of pseudo-science:

Many good things may be said of Dr More, as a pious Christian, and of great abilities. But he was a Babylonian philosopher and divine, a bigot to the Cartesian system, knew nothing deeper than an hypothesis, nor truer of the nature of the soul than that which he has said of its pre-existence, which is little better than that foolish brat descended from it, the transmigration of souls. I know no other name for his "Divine Dialogues" than a jumble of learned rant, heathenish babble, and gibberish, dashed or heated here and there with flashes of piety. What you have seen of his severity against the light within (which is in other words, God within), is sufficient to determine his character with you.[38]

Law's contribution to the tradition he valued was corrective; he sought to provide a reasoned argument for the light within which would guarantee it from aberration and perversion.

Perhaps the most striking aspect of Law's approach to this problem is his measured and sympathetic treatment of 18th century Quakerism.

[36] Diary, 16 April 1737, Remains, II, 112. The identification in the popular mind of Quietism and Quakerism is revealed in a translation of Bossuet's *Relation sur le Quiétisme* which appeared as a shilling pamphlet at the turn of the century. The pamphlet bore the catching title *Quakerism à la Mode: or A History of Quietism, particularly that of the Lord Archbishop of Cambray and Madame Guyone. Done into English* (London: J. Harris and A. Bell, 1698). The writer of the preface argues that "the controversy of Quietism" means that the Church of Rome can no longer boast of her unity, "that Quakerism owes its origin to that anti-Christian Church and, that their opinions are much favoured there at present."

[37] Law, Letter, quoted in Overton, pp. 407–8. The Philadelphian Society was kept going for only six years (1697–1703).

[38] Law, Letter, quoted in *ibid.*, p. 416.

Naturally uneasy, as a high-church non-juror, about the nature of Quakerism, he nevertheless chose not to publish a prepared critique of Quakerism in his *Demonstration of the Gross and Fundamental Errors of a Late Book, called "A Plain Account of the Sacrament of the Lord's Supper"* (1737).[39] This attack on the latitudinarian school of Hoadly was thus appreciated by high-churchmen without provoking the Quakers.[40] Byrom and Law were naturally attracted to Quakerism, and on one occasion Law teasingly suggested that Byrom was proselytising for the sect.[41] It is probable that by 1737 Byrom and Law were aware that the cause of real Christianity would only be advanced by a renewal of the forces latent in quietism and Quakerism. In the years immediately preceding the rise of Evangelicalism, Byrom and Law were feeling around for allies in the task of distinguishing Light and Enlightenment, real and nominal Christianity.

By 1739 the renewal was underway. Byrom notes the beginnings of religious revival in his diary, and is, with Law, closely involved in the context of its occurrence. In 1736 Byrom had brought to Law's attention the case of Fanny Henshawe, a Quaker who challenged the Church of England in the person of Law to show good reason why she should not remain a Quaker. Byrom quotes her as writing:

> Notwithstanding I know it's the general opinion of the profession of the Church of England that miracles are now ceased, yet I go first to one of the most worthy professors of this Church, to try if God will please through his assistance to give deliverance and free me from mine enemy... Otherwise I must seek a remedy from the fountain of my affliction, and with Naimon be glad to wash in the river I disdained, and thereby experience who are the true prophets in Israel.[42]

In the same letter, Byrom instances Mme Guion as an example of the current confusion between Quakerism and quietism.[43] The critique of the established church was gathering momentum; the alliance, or confusion, between Quakerism and quietism was the symptom of a growing need that was met with the rise of evangelicalism.

These various trends coalesce in the person of Josiah Martin, a

[39] Hoadly was the author of this "late book". See S. H. Hobhouse, *William Law and 18th Century Quakerism* (London: Allen and Unwin, 1927), p. 230.

[40] For an account of Law's drafts against Quakerism, see *ibid.*, pp. 205–34.

[41] See Law's remark to Byrom, following the latter's mismanagement of the Fanny Henshawe affair: "Well, have you made any more Quakers?" Diary, 13 April 1737. *Remains*, II, 105.

[42] J. Byrom to W. Law, 21 December 1736, quoted in Hobhouse, *William Law and 18th Century Quakerism*, p. 135. This letter was not printed in Byrom's *Remains*.

[43] See *ibid.*, p. 137.

Quaker and editor of French quietists.[44] In the preface to the second edition of his translation of Fénelon in 1739, he notes, with some justification, that "the rising heresy, which they call Quietism" is in fact "a modern nickname for old Christianity."[45] Martin was in a position to know; a friend of Zinzendorf, he went on to espouse the cause of the Moravians and Methodists. Byrom corroborates Martin's claim. He notes the Moravian phenomenon in June 1738: "There is much talk about Moravians and many persons who have been moved by them to a Christian turn of thought and life."[46] The quietism of the Moravians he is prepared to accept as a modern expression of old Christianity. He is less categorical in his first reference to the Methodists in February 1739,[47] and by April 1739 it becomes clear that Byrom has had a difference of opinion with Charles Wesley.[48] But his enthusiasm for the Moravians continues unabated, and in April 1739 he finds himself in "a room full of Germans and English," including Zinzendorf and Josiah Martin.[49]

Byrom thus registers the part played by the coming together of Quakerism and Quietism in the origins of the Evangelical Revival. Five years later, Byrom received a visit from a man who "sat with us a little and told us of his brothers turning Methodists or Moravians, that his mother was born a Quaker."[50] There is a wry humour about this incident, which so aptly reflects the fortunes of a Quietist tradition superseded by an evangelical revival which it desired but was incapable of engendering.

At the outset Byrom identified himself with the Moravians, and preserved his distances with respect to the Methodists. Thus in June 1739 he notes with some coolness the remarkable results obtained by George Whitefield's open-air preaching:

Mr Whitefield preaches away at Blackheath etc.; he is the chief topic of private conversation... He had lords, dukes etc., to hear him at Black-

[44] Josiah Martin (1683–1747) is best remembered for his reply (1741) to Voltaire's account of English Quakerism. For a description of Josiah Martin's writings, see *ibid.*, pp. 155–7.

[45] Quoted in *ibid.*, p. 157.

[46] J. Byrom to Mrs Byrom, 15 June 1738, *Remains*, II, 207.

[47] "I having said in the vestry that I was no Methodist, and Mr Stonehouse that I was taken for one, ... Mr Rivington, I think it was, told him that one of them had said that there was no true doctrine preached since Oliver's time." Diary, 16 February 1739, *ibid.*, II, 228, 234.

[48] J. Byrom to his son, 26 April 1739, *ibid.*, II, 241. The difference sprang from the Wesleys' condemnation of mysticism.

[49] *Ibid.*, II, 242.

[50] Diary, 22 January 1744, *ibid.*, II, 376.

heath, who gave guineas and half-guineas for his orphan house; he does surprising things, and has a great number of followers both curious and real. This field preaching, they say, is got into France as well as Germany, England, Scotland, Wales, etc. People are more and more alarmed at the wonder of it, but none offer to stop it that I hear of.[51]

A fortnight later Byrom came across the notorious Mr Whitefield in person, and reported the incident to his wife:

While we were there came in the so much talked of Mr Whitefield, and company with him... I am surprised at the progress which he has made, to which the weakness of his printing adversaries does not a little contribute... Thou wilt bid me again, perhaps, not mind anything about him; I do it very little, but the subject which he has raised so much attention to is very well worth minding.[52]

Byrom's curiosity in these matters gets the better of his wife's advice; but it is "the subject which he has raised" rather than Whitefield's success that Byrom commends, and he considers that the Moravians serve the interests of real Christianity more than the Methodists.[53] Indeed as early as September 1739 an associate of Zinzendorf solicits Byrom's help in translating some of his leader's writings.[54]

It must not be overlooked that, before the beginnings of Methodism, Byrom had met Charles Wesley in his capacity as fellow high-churchman, and had received an impression which was to mark his attitude to Methodism all his life:

Mr Charles Wesley called as I was shaving, and brought two letters about the mystics that he had mentioned – one from his brother in Georgia, the other an answer to it from the brother at Tiverton, and both of them unintelligible to me... I wondered where Mr John Wesley had got his notions from... He defined the mystics to be those who neglected the use of reason and the means of grace – a pretty definition! ... I ... thought that neither of the brothers had any apprehension of mystics, if I had myself.[55]

The Wesleys' position on mysticism marks their departure from the central tendency of quietism. Byrom and Law, however, were not prepared to jettison their mystical insights in favour of a purely scriptural holiness. The gap was unbridgeable. Byrom could get the

[51] J. Byrom to Mrs Byrom, 14 June 1739, *ibid.*, II, 245–6.

[52] J. Byrom to Mrs Byrom, 28 June 1739, *ibid.*, II, 249.

[53] In the years following his meeting with Zinzendorf, Byrom was in close touch with the Moravian community. See *ibid.*, II, 319.

[54] J. C. Jacobi to J. Byrom, 5 September 1739, *ibid.*, II, 281.

[55] Diary, 2 July 1737, *ibid.*, II, 181. John is the brother in Georgia and Samuel the one in Tiverton.

Wesleys to publish a couple of his translations from Mlle Bourignon, but he could not prevent them prefacing their collection of hymns with an astute attack on the whole mystical and quietist tradition.[56]

There is no doubt that while the Moravian movement was a transitional one, with strong roots in the quietist tradition, the Methodist movement constituted a new departure, and one towards which the sympathies of Byrom and Law were severely limited. The Wesleys, unlike the Quietists, would not stay still; indeed they systematically stirred up people in all the corners of the kingdom. Byrom and Law on the other hand committed themselves to a less popular spirituality, and found themselves as stranded as the Quaker mother whose sons turned Methodist or Moravian.

[56] Byrom records the publication of the first Methodist Hymn Book as follows: "They have both together printed a book of hymns, amongst which they have inserted two of Mrs Bourignon's ... They have introduced them by a preface against what they call mystic writers, ... for whom they say they had once a great veneration, but think themselves obliged ... to acknowledge their error and to guard others against the like." J. Byrom to his son, 26 April 1739, *ibid.*, II, 242. See also E. W. Baker, *A Herald of the Evangelical Revival* (London: Epworth Press, 1948), p. 42.

CHAPTER TEN

THEOLOGICAL RENEWAL

Having related Byrom and Law to their intellectual milieu, we can the better appreciate the originality and significance of the philosophy Law developed and Byrom versified. Although primarily derived from Boehme, as an instrument to sharpen his critique of latitudinarianism, it became in Law's hands a vision of life as well as a method of reasoning. Designed to support his theological views, it became a tool to render coherent all phenomenon, physical, psychological and spiritual. Its organic structure and its comprehensive application is such that it often reveals aesthetic implications. Although Law did not concern himself with following up these implications, their similarity in many respects to the Coleridgean aesthetic is striking and worthy of analysis.

To take a simple example; in a passage on the doctrine of the Trinity, Law concludes:

> We thus know the Trinity in ourselves... Without this knowledge, all the Scripture will be used as a dead letter, and formed only into a figurative, historical system of things, that has no ground in Nature, and learned Divines can only be learned in the explication of phrases, and verbal distinctions. The first chapter of Genesis will be a knot that cannot be untied; the mysteries of the Gospel will only be called federal rites, and their inward ground reproached as enthusiastic dreams.[1]

On the purely theological level, Law has developed an argument which revalues the Trinity at a time when this particular doctrine was the subject of interminable dispute, as almost the only article of faith separating deist from modernist. But Law goes on to relate the Trinity to its "ground in Nature," thus undermining the sterile confrontation of natural and revealed religion, and to its "inward ground," thus characterizing his opponents as pedants and hunters of enthusiasts. As we shall see, Law persistently develops his arguments along these

[1] *Appeal to All that Doubt*, Law, VI, 82.

lines, relating all his polemic to the firm ground that is both natural and inward. The accumulative effect is that he builds up a structure of thought which is, in its theological, psychological and potentially aesthetic content, diametrically opposed to the accepted orthodoxy of his age.

It is instructive to compare Law's revision of the doctrine of the Trinity with Berkeley's. Berkeley, like Law, is at odds with the prevailing fashion. Like Law, he wants to rescue the doctrine from the sterile controversy to which the "minute philosophers" have subjected it. Like Law, he writes of an "operative" or "active principle" which transcends the categories of Locke's theory of ideas. And like Law, he anticipates the findings of Coleridgean aesthetics. But, whereas Law appeals to his metaphysically defined "ground in Nature," Berkeley rests his case on the axiomatic and undefined ground of prudence and common sense.

Thus Law goes on to explain what he means by his "ground in Nature":

> Fire, and light, and air in this world are not only a true resemblance of the Holy Trinity in unity, but are the Trinity itself in its most outward, lowest kind of existence or manifestation; for there could be no fire, fire could not generate light, air could not proceed from both, these three could not be thus united, and thus divided, but because they have their root and original in the Triunity of the Deity.[2]

Berkeley on the other hand begins his revision of the doctrine of the Trinity with a critique of the Royal Society theory of language:

> Euphranor: It seems also to follow that there may be another use of words besides that of marking and suggesting distinct ideas, to wit, the influencing our conduct and actions... Whence it should seem to follow that those words which denote an active principle, soul, or spirit, do not, in a strict and proper sense, stand for ideas. And yet they are not insignificant neither; since I understand what is signified by the term *I*, or *myself*, or know what it means, although it be no idea, not like an idea, but that which thinks, and wills, and apprehends ideas, and operates about them.[3]

Berkeley is thus moving, with Law, towards a Coleridgean analysis of the inadequacies of Wilkins and Locke.

Berkeley goes on to argue that "to attain a precise simple abstract idea of number is as difficult as to comprehend any mystery in religion," and suggests that "we shall find it as difficult to form an idea of force

[2] *Ibid.*, VI, 118.
[3] Berkeley, p. 292.

as of grace."[4] Having poured cold water on some of the basic assumptions of his age, he feels he can restate the doctrine of the Trinity in terms which will be acceptable to intellectual prudence, common sense and moral reality:

Whence it seems to follow that a man may believe the doctrine of the Trinity, if he finds it revealed in Holy Scripture that the Father, the Son, and the Holy Ghost, are God, and that there is but one God, although he does not frame in his mind any abstract or distinct ideas of trinity, substance or personality; provided that this doctrine of a Creator, Redeemer, and Sanctifier makes impressions on his mind, producing therein love, gratitude, and obedience, and thereby becomes a lively operative principle, influencing his life and actions, agreeably to that notion of saving faith which is required in a Christian.[5]

Berkeley then is not jettisoning the thought-categories of his age. He is merely simplifying them to meet the dictates of common sense. Thus he relies on Locke's theory of the mind receiving impressions, without accepting the generally held implications of this. Berkeley is trying to interpret the Trinity as a moral reality. Law on the other hand sees the reality of the Trinity in the context of his metaphysical system. Both are attempting to salvage a Christian truth from the sterile verbal polemics of their age.

Since Law's thought is principally conceived as an instrument to revitalise the decadent condition of theology, it is important to understand how Law approached those theological problems he was prepared to tackle. There are three theological issues which Law dealt with in some detail, and they are all inseparable from the general structure of his thought. They can be referred to technically as a theology of the Fall, a theology of the Atonement, and a theology of Creation.

Law's originality as a theologian lies in his refusal to pronounce on either the Fall or the Atonement outside the context of the Creation. From this theological originality stems his latent aesthetic originality. For Law interprets the Fall and the Atonement in terms of the limited circle of man's nature; and man's own will, desire and imagination, not some exterior historical, figurative or cosmological force, comprise the categorical imperative of theological praxis.

Thus Law asserts "this Eternal Truth; namely that no being can rise higher than its own life reaches. The circle of the birth of life in

[4] *Ibid.*, pp. 293, 295.
[5] *Ibid.*, p. 297.

every creature is its necessary circumference, and it cannot possibly reach any further."[6] This is an interesting variant to the Augustan commonplace that the proper study of mankind is man. The measure of its variance and resemblance to the spirit of the Enlightenment can be gauged by referring to Law's chief source, Boehme. In Boehme's words:

Man is the great mystery of God, the microcosm, or the complete abridgment of the whole universe. He is the *mirandum Dei opus*, God's masterpiece, a living emblem and hieroglyphic of eternity and time; and therefore to know whence he is and what his temporal and eternal being and well being are, must needs be that one necessary thing, to which all our chief study should aim.[7]

Pope of course meant something different when he was apparently saying the same thing, and there is no doubt that the ideas of Law and Boehme were in their own context far removed from the spirit of the age. In the 18th century, theodicies were based on the argument from design, and nature meant first and foremost cosmos and landscape. Thus while 18th century theology argued over historical and cosmological evidence, Law started with man's nature.

In his *Spirit of Prayer* (1749–50), Law offered a critique of Bishop Sherlock's legalistic account of the Fall.[8] In Law's view, "all the laborious volumes on God's imputing Adam's sin to his posterity, ought to be considered as waste paper."[9] Sherlock and the modernists interpreted Adam's Fall as figurative death, a punishment from God, which they understood anthropomorphically as a legal transaction. In this way the real sense of the Fall in terms of man's condition was obscured. As Byrom put it in his versification of Law's *Spirit of Prayer*:

Without acknowledging that Adam died,
Scripture throughout is, in effect, denied;
All the whole process of Redeeming Love,
Of Life, of Light and Spirit from above,
Loses by Learning's piteous pretence
Of Modes and Metaphors its real sense.
All the glad tidings in the Gospel found
Are sunk in empty and unmeaning sound.[10]

[6] *Appeal to All that Doubt*, Law, VI, 81.

[7] Jacob Boehme, *The Signature of All Things* (London: J. M. Dent, 1912). Preface to the Reader, p. 3.

[8] Thomas Sherlock (1678–1761), Bishop of London from 1748, was the chief official spokesman against Hoadly in the Bangorian Controversy. In *The Use and Intent of Prophecy* (1725, 2nd ed. revised 1749) he refuted Whiston's Arian tendencies in particular and the Deists in general, adding an appendix entitled "An Enquiry into the Mosaic Account of the Fall." This provoked a rejoinder from Conyers Middleton as well as from Law. *DNB*

[9] Law, VII, 14. Quoted in *Poems*, II, 139.

[10] "An Epistle to a Gentleman of the Temple" (1749), lines 373–80, *Poems*, II, 161.

Moreover, in the eyes of Byrom and Law, Sherlock and the modernists were watering down the Christian interpretation of man. By minimising the extent of the Fall, they were placing a low value on the power of grace, retreating from theology, and inviting further incursions from the camp of the deists.[11] Byrom concludes his verses by identifying Sherlock and those who cavil over the nature of the Fall with the devil himself.[12] The refusal of Byrom and Law to compromise over the Fall seems to have been appreciated by at least one deist whose opinion law reported to Byrom.[13]

The way in which Byrom and Law related the Fall to the nature of man can be seen in one of Byrom's best lyrics, "On the Origin of Evil." Evil, says Byrom, is no external force to be minimised or explained away by legalistic formulae or cosmological theodicy:

Evil if rightly understood
Is but the skeleton of good
Divested of its flesh and blood.[14]

So runs the first verse which defined man's condition in terms not all that different from those of Leibnizian theodicy. But Byrom is no disciple of Pope and he goes on to assert that Christianity meets this condition by offering the flesh and blood of regenerated life. Having elaborated the implications of man's nature in its lapsed state, Byrom completes the circle in his last verse:

And when the life of Christ in men
Revives its faded image, then
Will all be paradise again.[15]

Evil and good then are part and parcel of man's nature. It follows that hell and heaven are likewise conditions of man, and not rewards and punishments meted out by some external power. Law persistently asks his readers to "consider this great truth":

You can be an inhabitant of no world, or a partaker of its life, but by its being inwardly the birth of your own life, or by having the nature and condition of that world born in you. And thus hell must be inwardly born in the soul, it must arise up within it ... before the soul can become an inhabitant of it.[16]

[11] See lines 381–6, *ibid.*
[12] See lines 463–76, *ibid.*, II, 165–6.
[13] See *Remains*, II, 516.
[14] *Poems*, II, 474.
[15] *Ibid.*, II, 475. Cf. Antoinette Bourignon who goes as far as claiming that Adam transmits grace as well as sin. Macewen, p. 92.
[16] *Appeal to All that Doubt*, Law, VI, 78.

In practical terms this merely confirms Law's position as a pietist or quietist, apostle of the interior life, such as he had revealed himself in his *Serious Call*. But Law launches his appeal for piety and the moral life from a total vision of man in his relation to God and the world, a vision which incorporates the old Renaissance insight of man as a microcosm.

Law follows a similar line of argument in his interpretation of the Atonement. In the second quarter of the 18th century, the old controversy between Arminians and Calvinists on the nature of the Atonement began to dominate the theological scene. This was largely due to the divergence of opinion among the evangelicals, between those who followed the traditional Calvinist view and Whitefield, and those who rallied behind the Wesleys' decision to take an Arminian stand. Byrom and Law were principally in disagreement with the Calvinist interpretation of the Atonement, for the Calvinists took a strictly legalistic view.

Law, who based his theology on the nature of man, saw that the issue turned on a mere preposition: "The whole truth therefore of the matter is plainly this, Christ given *for us*, is neither more nor less, than Christ given *into us*."[17] This view was anathema to the Calvinists, and one of their chief spokesmen, James Hervey, retorted with an attack on those who "are all for the sanctifying influence of the Spirit, and reckon this affiance on the Saviour's merits among the beggarly elements of religion." Hervey's quarrel with the like of Byrom and Law is that "they scarce ever mention, what Christ has done *for us*, but insist wholly upon what he does *in us*."[18]

Byrom took part in the controversy with "The Potter and his Clay," a verse by verse parody of Watts's "Behold the Potter and the Clay." In his poem Byrom substituted Arminian views for Calvinist ones.[19] And in his last long poem, "On Jonathan Edwards' Enquiry Concerning Free Will," Byrom returned to this problem. Here he displays a certain impatience with the whole controversy which had dragged

[17] *Spirit of Love*, Law, VIII, 99. Quoted in *Poems*, II, 476.

[18] James Hervey, *Theron and Aspasia* (1755), in *Works* (Newcastle: M. Brown, 1789), p. 129. It is Hervey who insists on the incompatibility of the two views. The nuance of Law's "into" for Hervey's "in" suggests an attempt to bridge the gap between immanence and transcendence. James Hervey (1714–58) came under the influence of the Oxford Methodists in 1733, but the Calvinism of *Theron and Aspasia* provoked a reply from John Wesley. Hervey's *Meditations and Contemplations* (1746), with its astute recipe of commonplace piety and high-flown preromanticism, was an 18th century best-seller, reaching its 25th edition in 1791. *DNB*

[19] See *Poems*, II, 509–13.

on for so long, and which the strength of Calvinism in the New World threatened to perpetuate. In similar strain to Watts, exasperated by the earlier endless controversy over the Trinity, he writes at the end of his tether:

> Well might I
> Be disappointed by a book so dry, –
> So sapless dry, – who cherish no opinion
> Of Calvinistic cobwebs, or Arminian!
> ....
> All Calvinistic or Arminian strain
> Is cobweb search.[20]

It is thus hardly surprising that Byrom and Law's commitment to Arminianism was never unconditional.

Law had in fact, as early as 1738, questioned the wisdom of Wesley's Arminian stand:

> Let me advise you not to be hasty in believing that because you change your language and expressions, you have changed your faith. The head can as easily amuse itself with a living and justifying faith in the blood of Jesus as with any other notion; and the heart, which you suppose to be a place of security, as being the seat of self-love, is more deceitful than the head.[21]

Law saw that Wesley was creating his own form of legalistic theology by insisting on the doctrine of justification, and that Wesley's reliance on the heart was as liable to abuse as any Calvinist interpretation of the Atonement. In all his contacts with the contemporary theology of the Atonement, Law maintained an organic theory in which regeneration was inseparable from the nature of man as conditioned by the Fall and the Creation.

Law based his theology of Creation on the theories of Boehme. These were presented in simplified form in several of Byrom's poems, notably in the one entitled "On the Union and Threefold Distinction of God, Nature and Creature." God is described as "free eternal light, or love, / Before, beyond all nature, and above," and as "Will / To

[20] *Ibid.*, II, 526, 529. This poem, written in 1762, appears as a letter to Mr Houghton in *Remains*, II, 639–42. For a discussion of Watts's exasperation, see John Hoyles, *The Waning of the Renaissance 1640–1740* (The Hague: Nijhoff, 1971), pp. 179–80. Jonathan Edwards (1703–58) was a New England Congregational theologian and philosopher, whose *Careful and Strict Enquiry into the Modern Prevailing Notions of that Freedom of Will which is supposed to be essential to Moral Agency, Vertue and Vice, Reward and Punishment, Praise and Blame* (1754) revealed him as the first great philosophic intelligence in American history. *DAB*

[21] Law to Wesley, 19 May 1738. Quoted in Overton, pp. 85–6.

every good."[22] Nature is described as "without Him ... the abyssal dark," and as "the attraction of desire, by want repelled":

> But by the Light's all-joyous power, the abyss
> Becomes the groundwork of a threefold bliss.[23]

And the Creation is described as "the gift of light and life / To Nature's contrariety and strife."[24] This is the basic framework of Law's thought.

In Byrom's verse the argument loses some of its force. It appears to be a mystical theology rather than an interpretation of the phenomenon of man. Law himself, however, is in no doubt that the theology interprets the phenomenon, and recapitulates the threefold nature of man in no uncertain terms:

> If man himself were not all these three things; viz. (1) A birth of the Holy Deity; (2) A birth of Eternal Nature, and (3) Also a Microcosm of all this great outward world; that is of everything in it, its stars and elements; and if the properties of every creaturely life were not in an hidden birth in him; no omnipotence of God could open the knowledge of divine and natural things in him.[25]

The syntax is significant; theology, or God's contact with man, is made to depend on an interpretation of man, and not vice versa. Both science (knowledge of natural things) and religion (knowledge of divine things) derive directly from a theology of Creation. God, Eternal Nature, and the World only have meaning as they are present in and to man. It is this system of thought which one can safely characterise as in diametrical opposition to the spirit of the age. As an infrastructure it possibly anticipates the subsequent development of existentialist theology and is certainly fraught with psychological and aesthetic implications which only become explicit with the advent of Blake, Coleridge and Wordsworth.

[22] *Poems*, II, 468.
[23] *Ibid.*, II, 469.
[24] *Ibid.* Byrom and Law have the same problem as the Cambridge Platonists; they want "the life of Nature" to "reflect the glories of the life of Grace," but in saying so have to add their inevitable refutal of Spinoza: "Nature is His, but Nature is not He." *Ibid.*, II, 470.
[25] *Way to Divine Knowledge*, Law, VI, 202.

CHAPTER ELEVEN

NATURE AND ENTHUSIASM

A vital link between Law's purely theological preoccupations and their consequent bearing on aesthetics can be found in his interpretation of those stock 18th century concepts, nature and enthusiasm. To Law's contemporaries these two concepts were opposites; each was invariably defined by way of the absence of the other. The originality of Law's thought is that they are identified, and a radically new set of opposites conceived. Thus for Byrom and Law, religious enthusiasm or divine illumination is the natural end of men, and the chief characteristic of man's nature which obstructs this end is human reason. Illumination is natural and reason unnatural. The argument is to all intents and purposes identical to that on which Romanticism came to be based.

Byrom summarised Law's argument in "A Contrast between Human Reason and Divine Illumination Exemplified in Three Different Characters" (c. 1753). The poem offers a critique of the major assumptions of 18th century thought. Byrom points out that

> Such words as nature, reason, common sense
> Furnish all writers with one same pretence.[1]

He goes on to describe common-sense reasoning, as exemplified by Bolingbroke, the combination of reasoning and intuition, as exemplified by William Hay,[2] and divine illumination, as exemplified by Boehme.[3] In fact Hay's intuition fell short of illumination, for he sought to deduce the principles of Christianity and morality from "a view of the universe."[4]

[1] *Poems*, II, 330.
[2] "Hay . . ./Gropes with his reason betwixt light and dark." *Ibid.*, II, 331.
[3] "Of Grace and Nature he explained the law." *Ibid.*
[4] William Hay (1695–1755) published in 1753 his *Religio Philosophi, or the Principles of Morality and Christianity, illustrated from a View of the Universe and of Man's Situation in it.*

Law, treating this issue with characteristic rigour, came to the conclusion that there was no half-way house between Bolingbroke and Boehme, and that as far as reasoning powers are concerned there was nothing to choose between the three of them:

What is the difference between reason in St Paul, a Spinosa, a Hobbes, or a Bolingbroke? None at all, or no other than in their outward shape. Therefore if reason be the divine image of likeness of God in man, a Hobbes and a Bolingbroke had as much of it as St Paul.[5]

The light of reason may be the common denominator in all men, but it is just because it has equal value in St Paul or Spinoza that it cannot be mistaken for the Candle of the Lord.[6] Reason is thus a faculty completely separate from, indeed opposite to, the image of God in man. And for Byrom and Law, the divine image constitutes the natural basis of illumination or enthusiasm.

Although Byrom and Law meant by nature something radically different from its generally accepted sense, there were points of contact. Law's reading of Newton, and his critique of Newton by the light of Boehme, illustrate the principal point of contact. Byrom, nearer than Law to the everyday pulse of the age, interpreted nature in an orthodox sense on at least one occasion, though with qualifications which link him to the tradition of Platonic idealism, rather than to the physico-theological school. Thus, considering nature as landscape, he writes:

If, when we cast a thoughtful, thankful eye
Towards the beauties of an evening sky,
Calm we admire, through the ethereal field,
The various scenes that even clouds can yield, –
What huge delight must Nature's fund afford,
Where all the rich realities are stored
Which God produces from its vast abyss
To own his glory and his creatures' bliss![7]

This particular effusion is built on the traditional dualism of the Platonic rhapsodists, where external nature and the cosmos are opposed to the more sublime ideal realities. It is this dualism which Law's philosophy sought to eliminate; but whenever Byrom brought the concept of nature into the context of prevailing trends, this dualism was bound to raise its head.

[5] *Short Confutation of Warburton*, Law, VIII, 105–6. Quoted in *Poems*, II, 330.
[6] This amounts to a reversal of the position taken up by the Cambridge Platonists.
[7] "Epistle to a Gentleman of the Temple," lines 215–22, *Poems*, II, 154.

The pervasive nature of this dualism may be conveniently illustrated from the writings of Dr George Cheyne (1671–1743), member of the Royal Society, frequently in the company of Byrom, and strangely enough the man who is credited with having brought the works of Boehme to the attention of Law.[8] Cheyne's eclecticism outdid that of Byrom. He argued against Locke, corresponded with Hume, and in his *Philosophical Principles of Religion Natural and Revealed* (1705–1715) came near to anticipating Law's theory of nature. Thus he declared:

> There is a perpetual analogy (physical not mathematical) running on in a chain through the whole system of creatures up to their Creator... The visible are the images of the invisible... If gravitation be the principle of the activity of bodies, that of reunion with their origin must by analogical necessity be the principle of action in spirits. ... The pure and disinterested love of God and of all his images in a proper subordination is the consummate perfection of Christianity.[9]

The linking of physical and divine by analogical necessity is an attempt to eradicate the traditional dualism, and yet the whole analogy is constructed on a basic dualism. Nature is physical nature, the chain of being, kept in place by gravity; and the description of the activity of the spirit is grafted on to fit the system.

In the 18th century it was commonplace to make analogies between the physical and the divine, between the laws of the world and the laws of God. It was far from common to do what Law did, identify physical and divine on the little world of man. The common reaction to Law's philosophy, even among his sympathisers, was one of bewilderment. Thus, for example, Thomas Patten, a great admirer of Law *qua* pietist, found it necessary to write to Byrom, disparaging Law's reliance on physical theory to prove his hypothesis of divine illumination.[10] Patten was ill-prepared by the intellectual milieu of his age for a philosophy which transcended the commonplace categories of physico-theological dualism. He could not see that Law was not, as were the physico-theological modernists, resting his case for religion on the ground of physics, but rather on the ground of human nature.

[8] See *Remains*, II, 363. According to Hobhouse, Law did not discover Boehme until 1736. *William Law and 18th Century Quakerism*, p. 268.

[9] Quoted in Overton, pp. 95–6.

[10] Thomas Patten to J. Byrom, 25 April 1761, *Remains*, II, 633–4. Patten (1714–90)) was a clergyman and author of *The Opposition between the Gospel of Jesus Christ and what is called the Religion of Nature* (1759).

Thus, for Byrom and Law, there was no distinction between natural and revealed religion. As usual Byrom explains this schematically and in terms of individual redemption:

> Then, true religion, call it by the name
> "Christian" or "Natural," is still the same, –
> From Christ derived as healer of the soul,
> Or Nature, made by his re-entrance whole;
> Who is in every man the enlightening ray,
> The faith and hope of love's redeeming day, –
> The only name or power that can assure
> Nature's religion, that is, Nature's cure.[11]

Law, on the other hand, in the tone of a manifesto, relates this insight not only to an individual's human nature, but to the total fabric of existence: "The Christian doctrine of the salvation of mankind by a birth of the Son and Holy Spirit of God in them, is not only written in Scripture, but in the whole state and frame of Nature, and of every life in this world."[12] Clearly this sort of metaphysical philosophy is not that with which Thomas Patten finds fault. Law is not, like Cheyne, creating an analogy between an individual's human nature and the physical cosmos. He is rather, as this quotation suggests, claiming that the regeneration of nature is an eternal and universal process, and that Christianity enables man to participate in this regeneration.

It is becoming clear that Law is using the word "nature" in a special sense. He goes on to claim that "revealed religion is nothing else but a revelation of the mysteries of nature."[13] He does not mean the cosmos, though he uses curious analogies from the mineral world to make his point:

> The Christian religion ... has its infallible proof from all Nature. Consider death, or the deadness that is in a hard flint, and you will see what is the eternal death of a fallen angel: the flint is dead, or in a state of death, because its fire is bound, compacted, shut up, and imprisoned; this is its chains and bonds of death: a steel struck against a flint will show you, that every particle of the flint consists of this compacted fire.[14]

Law's conception of natural religion is remote indeed from that commonly accepted by the 18th century:

[11] "A Friendly Expostulation with a Clergyman Concerning the Redemption of Mankind," *Poems*, II, 479.
[12] *Appeal to All that Doubt*, Law, VI, 85.
[13] *Ibid.*, VI, 88.
[14] *Ibid.*, VI, 89.

For if there is but one thing that is life, and one thing that is death throughout all Nature, from the highest angel to the hardest flint upon earth, then, it must be plain, that the life which is to be raised or restored by religion, must, and can only be restored according to Nature.[15]

And it soon becomes clear that the equation between revealed and natural religion depends on a prior equation between nature and eternal nature: "When I speak of Nature as the ground and foundation of religion, I mean nothing like that which you call the religion of human reason, or Nature; for I speak here of Eternal Nature."[16]

Here we have the core of Law's thought. Significantly he is less concerned to erect an abstract philosophical system than to delineate a logic of regeneration based on the proposition that "there is life which belongs to death, and there is life which isn't death."[17] In his *Appeal to All that Doubt*, Law is persuasively categorical:

Salvation is a birth of life, but reason can no more bring forth this birth, than it can kindle life in a plant or animal. You might as well write the word flame, upon the outside of a flint, and then expect that its imprisoned fire should be kindled by it, as to imagine, that any images, or ideal speculations of reason painted in your brain, should raise your soul out of its state of death, and kindle the divine life in it. No: would you have fire from a flint; its house of death must be shaken, and its chains of darkness broken off by the strokes of a steel upon it. This must of all necessity be done to your soul, its imprisoned fire must be awakened by the sharp strokes of steel, or no true light can arise in it.[18]

When he does set this argument in the context of his metaphysical system, the system itself, taken from Boehme, ceases to be abstract and obscurantist, and becomes, in the central passage of *The Spirit of Love*, the clearest and most coherent definition of Law's vision of nature.

The whole structure of Law's thought depends on this vision of nature, which remains a vision in spite of an agglomeration of forbidding scholastic terms and distinctions. The central passage in which Law defines this vision runs as follows:

Nature, whether eternal or temporal, is that which comes not into being for its own self, or to be that which it is in itself, but for the sake of something that it is not, and has not. And this is the reason why Nature is only a desire; it is because it is for the sake of something else; and it is also the

[15] *Ibid.*
[16] *Ibid.*, VI, 98.
[17] D. H. Lawrence, *Women in Love* (London: Penguin Books, 1960), p. 208.
[18] Law, VI, 94.

reason why Nature in itself is only a torment, because it is only a strong desire, and cannot help itself to that which it wants, but is always working against itself.

Now a desire that cannot be stopped, nor get that which it would have, has a threefold contrariety, or working in it, which you may thus conceive, as follows. The first and peculiar property, or the one only will of the desire, as such, is to have that which it has not; and all that it can do towards having it is to act as if it were seizing it; and this is it which makes the desire to be a magic compressing, inclosing, or astringing; because that is all that it can do towards seizing of that which it would have. But the desire cannot thus magically astringe, compress, or strive to inclose, without drawing and attracting. But drawing is motion, which is the highest contrariety and resistance to compressing, or holding together. And thus the desire, in its magical working, sets out with two contrary properties, inseparable from one another, and equal in strength; for the motion has no strength but as it is the drawing of the desire; and the desire only draws in the same degree as it wills to compress and astringe; and therefore the desire, as astringing, always begets a resistance equal to itself. Now from this great and equally-strong contrariety of the two first properties of the desire, magically pulling, as I may say, two contrary ways, there arises, as a necessary birth from both of them, a third property, which is emphatically called a wheel, or whirling anguish of life. For a thing that can go neither inward nor outward, and yet must be and move under the equal power of both of them, must whirl, or turn round; it has no possibility of doing any thing else, or of ceasing to do that. And this whirling contrariety of these inseparable properties is the great anguish of life, and may properly be called the hell of Nature; and every lesser torment which any man finds in this mixed world has all its existence and power from the working of these three properties: for life can find no troublesome motions, or sensibility of distress, but so far as it comes under their power, and enters into their whirling wheel... This whirling anguish of life is a third state... The fourth, called fire, the fifth, called the form of light and love, and the sixth, sound, or understanding, only declare the gradual effects of the entrance of the Deity into the three first properties of Nature, changing, or bringing their strong wrathful attraction, resistance, and whirling, into a life and state of triumphing joy, and fulness of satisfaction; which state of peace and joy in one another is called the seventh property, or state of Nature.[19]

Law may not rate very highly as a philosopher, but the importance to religion, psychology and aesthetics of this radically new interpretation of the stock 18th century concept of nature has surely not received enough attention.

There is much here that is prophetic. Law anticipates Blake's proverb, "without contraries is no progression"; his "great anguish of life" anticipates the Romantic Agony and the angst of the Ex-

[19] Law, VIII, 17–20.

istentialists. His basic equation of nature with desire, the consequent description of life as "attraction, resistance and whirling" in what he calls the "hell of nature," and his attempt to apply a solution which will fulfil man's deepest needs and bring him back to "a state of nature" – all this anticipates the discoveries of Freud, and in particular the psycho-analytical concept of repression. The structure of Law's thought presupposes the unity of human nature and eternal nature. The Romantics, alienated by the dualism which separated man from landscape and the cosmos, sought a similar vision of a unitive nature in their art.

The 18th century was not indifferent to Law's strange ideas. He was from the beginning branded as an enthusiast; and for the 18th century, from Dr Johnson to Wesley, enthusiasm was nature's archetypal aberration, to be resisted at all costs. Law was in fact considered to be outside the pale of 18th century culture. A brief glimpse of the furious and far from urbane reaction his writings provoked, will confirm his isolation from the spirit of his age.

In 1726, a Mrs S.O., presumably an actress of some standing, published a pamphlet entitled *Law Outlawed; or, a Short Reply to Mr Law's Long Declamation against the Stage, wherein the wild rant, blind passion, and false reasoning of that piping-hot Pharisee are made apparent to the meanest capacity.* In it she declared: "I never read a more unfair reasoner. He begs the question. He is a madman who rails at theatres till he foams again."[20] A generation later, in 1762, Warburton replete with bishopric, launched a final broadside at Law. Law had died in 1761, but nothing daunted Warburton, in his *Doctrine of Grace*, pursued his victim beyond the grave. In the following *locus classicus* of the Augustan spirit, he accuses Law of being the ring-leader of a Behmenist sect, a disturber of the peace and a vulgar fanatic:

The leader of the sect amongst us, though manifesting an exemplary abhorrence of all carnal impurity, has fallen into the lowest dregs of spiritual. When I reflect on his wonderful infatuation, who has spent a long life in hunting after, and with an incredible appetite devouring the trash dropped from every species of mysticism, it puts me in mind of what travellers tell us of a horrid fanaticism in the East, where the devotee makes a solemn vow never to taste of other food than what has passed through the entrails of some impure or savage animal. Hence their whole lives are passed (like Mr Law's among his ascetics) in woods and forests, far removed from the converse of mankind.[21]

[20] Quoted in Overton, p. 41.

[21] Quoted in *ibid.*, p. 380. Notice how Warburton sublimates his fury into animal imagery; Gibbon on the same theme was less hysterical thanks to irony. Warburton became Bishop of Gloucester in 1760.

Warburton was merely uttering the consensus of the tribe; he had the support of a solid phalanx of bishops for whom enthusiasm was anathema.[22]

Law's entrance into this particular fray was provoked in the first instance by Dr Trapp's *Discourses on the Nature, Folly, Sin and Danger of being Righteous overmuch* (1739).[23] Taking the bull by the horns, Law returned the charge of enthusiasm against his opponents, and indeed against all the distinguished exponents of 18th century culture:

> Even the poor species of Fops and Beaux have a right to be placed among Enthusiasts, though capable of no other flame than that which is kindled by Tailors and Peruke-Makers. All refined Speculatists, are great Enthusiasts; for being devoted to the exercise of their imaginations, they are so heated into a love of their own ideas that they seek no other summum bonum. The Grammarian, the Critic, the Poet, the Connoisseur, the Antiquary, the Philosopher, the Politician, are all violent Enthusiasts, though their heat is only a flame from straw, and therefore they all agree in appropriating Enthusiasm to religion.[24]

The similarity in tone with the satiric touch of Swift and Pope is no accident. Law follows in their path as he lashes out with savage but urbane indignation at the host of little men who reflect an impoverished culture. Not even the deists escape his comprehensive charge; as he points out, "a Tindal and a Collins are as inflamed with the notions of infidelity as a St Bennet and St Francis with the doctrines of the Gospel."[25]

Byrom, for his part, in a long paraphrase, versifies Law with great zest and more than usual eloquence, producing here and there a couplet worthy of comparison with Pope:

> The sprightlier infidel, as yet more gay,
> Fires off the next ideas on his way, –
> The dry fag-ends of every obvious doubt;
> And puffs and blows for fear they should go out.
> . . . .
> To his own reason loudly he appeals, –

[22] Edmund Gibson (1669–1748), Bishop of London, author of *A Pastoral Letter against Lukewarmness and Enthusiasm* (1739); George Lavington (1684–1762), Bishop of Exeter, author of *The Enthusiasm of Methodists and Papists Compared* (1749–51, in three parts), and of *The Moravians Compared and Detected* (1755); and Richard Hurd (1720–1808), Bishop of Worcester, author of *An Assize Sermon on the Mischiefs of Enthusiasm and Bigotry* (1752). See *DNB* and A. W. Ward's introduction to Byrom's *Enthusiasm*, *Poems*, II, 173.

[23] Law replied with *An Earnest and Serious Answer to Dr Trapp's Discourse* (1740), followed in the same year by *An Appeal to All that Doubt* and *Some Animadversions on Dr Trapp's Reply.*

[24] *Some Animadversions*, Law, VI, 307–8.

[25] *Ibid.*, VI, 308–9.

No saint more zealous for what God reveals!
Think not that you are no enthusiast, then!
All men are such, as sure as they are men.
. . . .
You need not go to cloisters or to cells,
Monks or field-preachers, to see where it dwells.
It dwells alike in balls and masquerades;
Courts, camps, and 'changes it alike pervades.
There be enthusiasts who love to sit
In coffee-houses, and cant out their wit.[26]

Byrom waxes particularly eloquent in his satire of Augustan classical learning:

One man politely, seized with classic rage,
Dotes on old Rome and its Augustan Age.
. . . .
Where does all sense to him and reason shine?
Behold, in Tully's rhetoric divine!
"Tully?" Enough; high o'er the Alps he's gone,
To tread the ground that Tully trod upon;
Haply, to find his statue or his bust,
Or medal greened with Ciceronian rust.[27]

Inevitably, special attention is paid to Warburton, author of a "Disquisition on Egyptian Hieroglyphics."[28] And it soon becomes clear that Byrom and Law's defence of religious enthusiasm is one expression of their concern to distinguish the light of the spirit from the enlightenment of the letter.

Thus Byrom, in a letter prefixed to his poem *Enthusiasm* (1752), claims that "there is a right enthusiasm as well as a wrong one," and notes of Law's opponents that

so long as they have only Light enough to hate Light, they may, upon the first glimpse of it, retire into their earthliness, and push out their works as thick as mole-hills. But, in reality, a single page proceeding from a right spirit, whose Enthusiasm they all despise, is worth a library of such a produce.[29]

[26] *Enthusiasm* (1752), lines 215–18, 223–6, 231–6, *Poems*, II, 189, 190.

[27] *Ibid.*, II, 182, 183 (lines 91–2, 107–12).

[28] Warburton's "Disquisition" appeared in his *Divine Legation* (1741). Law had referred to the man "whose heated brain is all over painted with ancient Hieroglyphics." *Some Animadversions*, Law, VI, 307. Byrom wittily paraphrases:

"Another's heated brain is painted o'er
With ancient hieroglyphic marks of yore;
He old Egyptian mummies can explain,
And raise 'em up almost to life again."

Enthusiasm, lines 127–30, *Poems*, II, 184.

[29] 3 September 1751, *Poems*, II, 169.

Byrom manages his mole conceit beautifully, and Law points the moral with Swift-like irony:

He that has gone thus high into the clouds, and dug thus deep into the dark for these glorious discoveries, may well despise those Christians as brainsick visionaries, who are sometimes finding a moral and spiritual sense in the bare letter and history of Scripture-facts.[30]

What is significant in Byrom and Law's defence of enthusiasm is that it prefigures Coleridge's defence of Bunyan and Boehme. Coleridge read in his copy of *Pilgrim's Progress* an anecdote from which he drew the following conclusion:

This is a valuable anecdote, for it proves, what might have been concluded a priori, that Bunyan was a man of too much genius to be a fanatic. No two qualities are more contrary than genius and fanaticism. Enthusiasm, indeed, is almost a synonym of genius; the moral life in the intellectual light, the will in the reason; and without it, says Seneca, nothing truly great was ever achieved by man.[31]

In like manner Coleridge exclaimed, "How dare I be ashamed of the Teutonic theosophist, Jacob Behmen?," and maintained that "Jacob Behmen was an enthusiast, in the strictest sense, as not merely distinguished, but as contra-distinguished, from a fanatic."[32] For Coleridge, poetic genius was not divorced from religious enthusiasm; and it is to Law's credit that, like Coleridge, he defined the moral life in terms of intellectual light, and the reason in terms of the will. Only a small step was needed to apply discoveries to the aesthetic field, and define genius in terms of enthusiasm.

[30] *Some Animadversions*, Law, VI, 307. Quoted in *Poems*, II, 184.

[31] S. T. Coleridge, *On the 17th Century*, ed. R. F. Brinkley (Durham, North Carolina: Duke University Press, 1955), p. 477. The anecdote, recorded by Bunyan's editor in a note, runs as follows:

"Bunyan wrote this precious book in Bedford Jail, where he was confined on account of his religion ... A Quaker came to the jail, and thus addressed him: 'Friend Bunyan, the Lord sent me to seek for thee, and I have been through several counties in search of thee, and now I am glad I have found thee.' To which Mr Bunyan replied: 'Friend, thou dost not speak the truth in saying the Lord sent thee to seek me; for the Lord well knows that I have been in this jail for some years; and if he had sent thee, he would have sent thee here directly.'" *Ibid.*, p. 476.

[32] S. T. Coleridge, *Biographia Literaria*, Chapter 9, p. 73.

CHAPTER TWELVE

PSYCHOLOGY AND AESTHETICS

The aesthetic implications of Law's thought become clearer still when an analysis is made of Byrom and Law's revaluation of traditional Enlightenment psychology. Their critique of Descartes and Locke stems from Law's theology of Creation. In their account of the nature of man, they merely spell out the psychological implications of this theology. In his "Thoughts on the Constitution of Human Nature as Represented in the Systems of Modern Philosophers," Byrom has perhaps Hutcheson particularly in mind; but through Hutcheson, he is attacking the sources of Enlightenment psychology, Descartes and Locke.[1]

Four verses of this poem are worth quoting in full, for they display in conveniently schematised form Byrom's distaste for a mechanical theory of human nature:

> Strong passions draw, like horses that are strong,
> The body-coach of flesh and blood along;
> While subtle reason, with each rein in hand,
> Sits on the box, and has them at command;
> Raised up aloft, to see and to be seen,
> Judges the track, and guides the gay machine.
> . . . .
> They who are loud in human reason's praise,
> And celebrate the drivers of our days,
> Seem to suppose, by their continual bawl,
> That passions, reason, and machine, is all;

[1] Hutcheson's *System of Moral Philosophy* was published posthumously in 1755. Vauvenargues claimed in 1746 that the true nature of man lay not in reason but in the passions. But, whether the passions or reason were given priority, a mechanical theory of psychology was the hall-mark of the Enlightenment. In 1734 Voltaire described the passions as follows: "It is with this motivating force that God, whom Plato called the eternal geometer, and whom I call the eternal machinist, has animated and embellished nature: the passions are the wheels which make all these machines go." Quoted in Ernst Cassirer, *The Philosophy of the Enlightenment* (Boston: Beacon Press, 1951), p. 107.

To them the windows are drawn up, and clear
Nothing that does not outwardly appear.

Matter and motion, and superior man
By head and shoulders, form their reasoning plan,
Viewed and demurely pondered, as they roll;
And scoring traces on the paper soul,
Blank, shaven white, they fill th' unfurnished pate,
With new ideas, none of them innate.

. . . .

Sense, reason, passions, and the like, are still
One self-same man, whose action is his will;
Whose will, if right, will soon renounce the pride
Of an own reason for an only guide;
As God's unerring spirit shall inspire,
Will still direct the drift of his desire.[2]

Byrom's allegory of the stagecoach does justice to the orthodox view that "passions, reason, and machine, is all." Descartes and Locke based their psychology, as they did their physics, on matter and motion, and the third verse quoted shows how Byrom felt it necessary to attack Locke's denial of innate ideas. Byrom and Law wanted to affirm the subjectivity of human nature, and make the soul more than a piece of paper. Arguing within the framework of mechanical psychology, Byrom sees the need to open the windows of the stagecoach and find an executive will inside.

In *Enthusiasm* Byrom dwells on this theme without resorting to allegory. Man may choose to be directed by one of three forces; either the passions, described as "clouds of sensual appetites" and "smothering lusts"; or the reason, described, as was Hay's reason, as a mediocre intuitive will-o'-the-wisp, which "from ideal glimmerings" raises "showy and faint, a superficial blaze," and leaves "untouched the things," able only to "creep round and round the names"; or the will, described lyrically as "the light / The love, the joy, that makes an angel bright."[3] Elsewhere Byrom equates the will with the spirit,[4] and with faith.[5] And it is clear that he has the same priority in mind when he exalts the heart above any other human faculty:

Love is to me the plainest word of all.
Plainest, – because that what I love, or hate,
Shows me directly my internal state;

[2] Stanzas 1, 4–5, 8, *Poems*, I, 240–2.
[3] Lines 275–84, *ibid.*, 192.
[4] Diary, 5 September 1739, *Remains*, II, 280.
[5] "On Faith, Reason and Sight," lines 63–4, *Poems*, II, 341.

By its own consciousness is best defined,
Which way the heart within me stands inclined.
....
Religion, then, is love's celestial force
That penetrates through all to its true source;
....
Not to the skies or stars; but to the part
That will be always uppermost, – the heart.[6]

In Byrom's formulation the critique of Descartes and Locke is made in the interests of giving first place to religious experience. On one occasion Byrom even includes the imagination in his list of minor and overrated faculties, thus contradicting his encomium on that faculty in *Enthusiasm*.[7] But this inconsistency is due to his straying from Law's own views on this matter.

In his series of answers to Trapp which appeared in 1740, Law sought to provide a definition of human nature which would support his theology of Creation and his revaluation of enthusiasm. In doing this he made it clear that the will, the spirit, and faith, were not mere signs of religious tendencies, revealing a piety which Trapp might well characterise as being "righteous overmuch"; they were, according to Law's argument, grounded in the very stuff of human nature, and could be more exactly characterised as will, imagination and desire.

With force and clarity Law eliminates the inconsistencies in Byrom's verses and declares:

In Will, Imagination and Desire consist the life, or fiery driving of every intelligent creature. And as every intelligent creature is its own self-mover, so every intelligent creature has power of kindling and enflaming its Will, Imagination and Desire, as it pleases, with shadows, fictions or realities; with things carnal or spiritual, temporal or eternal. And this kindling of the Will, Imagination and Desire, when raised into a ruling degree of life is properly that which is to be understood by Enthusiasm.[8]

That there may be no doubt as to the identification of imagination and desire with the will, Law makes a point of reinstating these faculties as central to the human constitution:

We are apt to think that our Imaginations and Desires may be played with, that they rise and fall away as nothing, because they do not always bring forth outward and visible effects. But indeed they are the greatest reality we have, and are the true formers and raisers of all that is real and

[6] "Divine Love the Essential Characteristic of True Religion," lines 2–6, 37–8, 41–2, *ibid.*, II, 416–18.

[7] See "Thoughts upon Human Reason," lines 41–8, *ibid.*, II, 338.

[8] *Some Animadversions*, Law, VI, 305–6. Quoted in *Poems*, II, 180.

solid in us. All outward power that we exercise in the things about us, is but a shadow in comparison of that inward power, that resides in our Will, Imagination and Desires; these communicate with eternity, and kindle a life which always reaches either heaven or hell. This strength of the inward man makes all that is the angel, and all that is the devil in us ... Now our Desire is ... always alive, always working and creating in us... It perpetually generates either life or death in us.[9]

This is the prophetic and pregnant paragraph which Byrom versifies in *Enthusiasm* as follows:

Imagination, trifling as it seems,
Big with effects, its own creation, teems.
We think our wishes and desires a play,
And sport important faculties away.
Edged are the tools with which we trifle thus,
And carve out deep realities for us.[10]

It is difficult to believe that Coleridge, who confessed his debt to Boehme and Law, could have missed the full force of this unique 18th century celebration of the imagination. Byrom and Law transcend the limitations of a preromantic taste for the sublime; the latent aesthetic they delineate is firmly geared to a revolutionary structure of thought which is similar to that developed by Blake, and is designed to establish a common ground for psychological and theological truth.

It is probable that Coleridge underestimated Byrom and Law because they belonged to a past with which Coleridge was still in direct contact.[11] The dominant feature of this recent past was the preromantic tradition, which never really escaped the grip of Newton and Locke; and, viewed from Coleridgean heights, Byrom and Law may well have been barely distinguishable from those preromantics who celebrated the imagination. There is even perhaps some justice in Coleridge's neglect, for Byrom and Law's definition of the imagination has affinities with some of the ideas of the preromantics. One can hardly ascribe to Byrom and Law a preromantic taste for the sublime, but one can note in some of the preromantics a tendency to take the imagination beyond the circle of fancy and use it to establish

[9] *Appeal to All that Doubt*, Law, VI, 134–5.

[10] Lines 37–42, *Poems*, II, 180. Ward has "our" for Chalmers' "out" in the last line.

[11] Cf. Cassirer, whose description of the limitations of Romanticism may be taken as corroborative evidence: "Romanticism, which is incomparably superior to the 18th century in the breadth of its historical horizon and its gift of the historical sense, loses its advantage in the very moment when its seeks to place this century in proper historical perspective. This movement ... fails to live up to its ideal when it encounters that past with which it is still in direct contact." Cassirer, p. 198.

a common ground for the fields of theology, psychology and aesthetics. The extent to which this tendency falls short of the Coleridgean position and differs from that taken by Byrom and Law, can be measured by referring to a few touchstones.

Coleridge's critique of preromanticism is based on his opposition to Newton and Locke. As such, it is at the same time theological and psychological, as well as aesthetic. He writes in a *locus classicus* of 1801:

> My opinion is this – that deep thinking is attainable only by a man of deep feeling, and that all truth is a species of revelation. The more I understand of Sir Isaac Newton's works, the more boldly I dare utter to my own mind, and therefore to you, that I believe the souls of 500 Sir Isaac Newtons would go to the making up of a Shakespeare or a Milton... Newton was a mere materialist – mind, in his system is always passive, – a lazy looker-on on an external world. If the mind be not passive, if it be indeed made in God's image, and that too in the sublimest sense – the image of the Creator – there is ground for suspicion, that any system built on the passiveness of the mind must be false, as a system.[12]

To the extent that the preromantics built a system, they built it on the passiveness of the mind, and any tendencies towards a Coleridgean position are conditioned by the dominance of Newton and Locke.

Mallet in 1728 celebrates the imagination in the context of Newtonian sublime:

> Companion of the Muse, creative power,
> Imagination! at whose great command
> Arise unnumbered images of things,
> Thy hourly offspring: thou, who canst at will
> People with air-born shapes the silent wood,
> And solitary vale, thy own domain,
> Where Contemplation haunts; oh come, invoked,
> To waft me on thy many-tinctured wing,
> O'er earth's extended space: and thence, on high,
> Spread to superior worlds thy bolder flight,
> Excursive, unconfined.[13]

This is the model for hosts of poetic flights in the preromantic idiom. The imagination may be a "creative power," but it is only a "companion of the Muse." It is one of Fancy's minions. It creates, not vision, but "images of things"; it inhabits, not its own world, but "earth's extended space." Its will does not shape things, but invents

[12] Letter to Thomas Poole, 23 March 1801. Coleridge, *On the 17th Century*, pp. 400–1.
[13] Mallet, *The Excursion*. Chalmers, XIV, 17.

the fictions of poetic mythology. It reflects the colours and prospects of landscape and the cosmos. Mallet's gestures of sublimity cannot hide his passive materialism and the fact that he is a "lazy looker-on on an external world."

In the 1740s Young and Akenside made important contributions to the development of preromantic aesthetics. And yet neither sought to abandon Locke's epistemology in an effort to redefine the imagination. Young indeed lived up to the second half of Coleridge's axiom that "deep thinking is attainable only by a man of deep feeling." Thus he called on his readers to "feel the great truths," and coined his own axioms: "To feel, is to be fired; / And to believe, Lorenzo! is to feel."[14] The intimations of a Wordsworthian aesthetic are unmistakable, and yet in another passage, which has rightly been compared to "Tintern Abbey," it is evident that Young is only celebrating the imagination to the extent that he is celebrating the senses, which

> Take in, at once, the landscape of the world,
> At a small inlet, which a grain might close,
> And half create the wondrous world they see.[15]

Young is making as much a scientific point as an aesthetic one. Vision is sensory vision; the object of vision is landscape. His "half create" has psychological affinities with the Wordsworthian aesthetic, but is far removed from Coleridge's definition of the imagination. This is because Young writes in the context of the epistemological tradition founded by Locke. He celebrates, not the imagination, but sense-impressions:

> Our senses, as our reason, are divine.
> But for the magic organ's powerful charm,
> Earth were a rude, uncoloured chaos, still.[16]

Like Mallet, Young implies that the imagination is a faculty which exercises itself in receiving sense-impressions from the visible universe.

Akenside is a little more sophisticated, at least in his theory. For him,

> there are certain powers in human nature which seem to hold a middle place between the organs of bodily sense and the faculties of moral perception; they have been called by a very general name, the Powers of

[14] Young, *Night Thoughts. Ibid.*, XIII, 434.
[15] *Ibid.*, XIII, 450.
[16] *Ibid.*

Imagination. Like the external senses, they relate to matter and motion; and at the same time, give the mind ideas analogous to those of moral approbation and dislike.[17]

Akenside thus allows imagination to take up a middle position between natural and moral philosophy. There can, however, be little but token autonomy here, for imagination is defined only in relation to the physics of Newton and the psychology of Locke, with a dash of Shaftesbury's moral sense to hold things together. Imagination is set fairly and squarely in the context of Enlightenment epistemology. It becomes almost a mechanically defined instrument acting as a vehicle between the sense perceptions and the moral sense.

Akenside did of course cultivate a certain autonomy of the imagination, but fell short of declaring its independence. Thus in his 1747 ode "To Caleb Hardinge," he reveals with gnomic precision just how far he was prepared to go on the road that leads from Locke to the Romantics:

Beauty with Truth I strive to join,
And grave assent with glad applause;
To paint the story of the soul,
And Plato's visions to control
By Verulamian laws.[18]

Akenside was prepared to indulge his imagination in the form of Platonic vision, as long as Baconian propriety was not offended.

It must be admitted that when in later years Akenside came to add a second book to his *Pleasures of the Imagination*, the Platonic vision tends to predominate and there is little Baconian control. To this extent Akenside moves away from Locke and towards Coleridge, but at the expense of sinking into a mystical gibberish. Thus he writes of

forms which never deigned
In eyes or ears to dwell, within the sense
Of earthly organs; but sublime were placed
In his essential reason, leading there
That vast ideal host which all his works
Through endless ages never will reveal.[19]

The Platonic jargon and pietistic content vitiate this passage's resemblance to Coleridge. In any case, Akenside is talking about the mind of God, not about man's imagination, and he is far from equating the two, or even making a useful analogy.

[17] Akenside, *The Pleasures of the Imagination* (1744), The Design. *Ibid.*, XIV, 59.
[18] Akenside, *Odes*. *Ibid.*, XIV, 108.
[19] Akenside, *The Pleasures of the Imagination* II (1765). *Ibid.*, XIV, 87.

Akenside indeed, taken with or without his Platonic rhapsodies, is solidly committed to Enlightenment epistemology. It is only fitting that he makes explicit reference to the aesthetic implications of Locke's new way of ideas. According to Akenside, "that various and complicated resemblance existing between several parts of the material and immaterial worlds, which is the foundation of metaphor and wit ... seems in great measure to depend on the early association of our ideas."[20] Akenside no more escapes the grip of Newton and Locke than do Mallet and Young. Wordsworth and Coleridge followed Akenside in experimenting with the aesthetics of associationism, but there is no sign in Akenside of the qualitative leap which Coleridge went on to make. In Akenside and the preromantics there is no way forward to a Coleridgean definition of the imagination, only occasional sorties into the cul-de-sac of the sublime. The preromantics were condemned to dig this delusive mine. It had its compensations and its premonitions of the revolution that had to come.[21] But for the preromantics, the imagination was an indulgence imprisoned in a hostile system, rather than the means of transforming that system. The context in which Byrom and Law wrote of the imagination constituted a new base, in which theological, psychological and aesthetic insights could be organically related to the little world of man. This new base was capable of sustaining the qualitative leap denied to the preromantics.

In formulating a definition of the imagination to support their critique of Descartes, Newton and Locke, Byrom and Law were closely adumbrating the formulae employed by Blake, Wordsworth and Coleridge to support a Romantic aesthetic. Four areas of definition common to Law and the Romantics can be distinguished and delineated.

[20] Akenside, *The Pleasures of the Imagination* (1744), The Design. *Ibid.*, XIV, 60.

[21] The compensation generally took the form of an indulgent celebration of the art of the bard (cf. the works of James Beattie). Such celebration even penetrates the tedious second-hand theodicy of Soame Jenyns, who wrote in a rash moment: "The rapid stream of eloquence / Bears all before it, passion, reason, sense ... / The bard's enchanting art, ... / Breathes all pathetic, lovely and sublime. ... / The poet gives us a creation new, / More pleasing and more perfect than the true. ... / The mind accepts the kind deceit, / And thence foresees a system more complete." *On the Immortality of the Soul* (1759), *ibid.*, XVII, 624. Jenyns exploits the preromantic taste for the sublime to compensate for the inadequacies of a Leibnizian theodicy.

Henry Brooke, on the other hand, is nearer Byrom in prefiguring the insights of Coleridge, when he writes towards the end of the preromantic period of "Spirits that, like their God, with mimic skill, / Produce new forms and images at will. ... / Thus, in the womb of man's abyss are sown / Natures, worlds, wonders, to himself unknown." *Redemption* (1772), *ibid*, XVII, 442. Here at least the Platonic content does not evaporate into rhapsody, and is related to theological, psychological and aesthetic considerations.

In the first place, there is the analogy between imagination and God. The psychological basis of such a claim is expressed in terms of spiritual need in Byrom's verse paraphrase of one of Boehme's epistles. Boehme had written: "The internal ground doth sigh and pant after the inflammation and motion of the light, and fain would have it; but the nature is able to do nothing."[22] And Byrom interpreted for the benefit of the 18th century:

> Thus the poor Soul, accounted for a fool
> By all the reasoners of a gayer school,
> By all the graver people who embrace
> Here verbal promises of future grace,
> Sighs from its deep internal ground, and pants
> For such enlightening comfort as it wants.[23]

In other words, human nature has a deep internal ground, neglected by Descartes and Locke, and unsatisfied by the panaceas of contemporary theologians. This is the inward ground on which Law sought to revalue the doctrine of the Trinity. With it he hopes to resolve the dichotomies of Cartesian dualism. In the reality of the inward ground the spirit's desire for God is such that it is endowed with a creative power. Like God, the imagination creates the basic realities out of itself, that is out of its sense of need, that is out of nothing.

In the work of Byrom the analogy between imagination and God has a tang of dogmatism about it, while in Law's hands it takes the form of a sustained and coherent argument. Thus Byrom formulates the theory of the inward ground in terms of the fire within:

> For flesh or spirit, wisdom from above,
> Or from this world an anger or a love,
> Must have its fire within the human soul.
> 'Tis ours to spread the circle or control.[24]

And he associates this fire with the operation of the Holy Spirit:

> Every good desire and thought
> Is in us by the Holy Spirit wrought.
> . . . .
> What is there left to sanctify the heart?
> "Reason and morals?" – And where live they most?
> In Christian comfort, or in Stoic boast?

[22] *The Epistles of Jacob Behmen* (1649), No. 14, quoted in *Poems*, II, 360.
[23] "A Letter from Jacob Behmen to a Friend," *ibid.*, II, 365.
[24] *Enthusiasm*, lines 271–4, *ibid.*, II, 192.

Reason may paint unpractised truth exact,
And morals rigidly maintain – no fact.[25]

The Holy Spirit is operative at the point where reason and morals are ineffective. But Law carries the logic of this formula beyond a nominal reliance on the third person of the Trinity, and concludes his argument with the Coleridgean formula:

Our own Will and desirous Imagination ... resemble in some degree the creating power of God, which makes things out of itself or its own working Desire.[26]

For Law, the imagination, and therefore God, is at the centre of the human condition. The inward ground, abolished by Descartes and Locke, is manifested through the faculty of the imagination, just as God is manifested in his creation. And in each case the creative activity involves no mere instrumentality of cause and effect, but an ongoing process of birth, rebirth, resurrection and regeneration.

The second way in which Byrom and Law formulate a Coleridgean definition of imagination is by asserting the subjectivity of human nature and distinguishing between two sorts of reason. It is Byrom who makes this point explicit. In "On Middleton Concerning Prophecy," he attacks those "wise freethinkers" who are

Resolved no other maxims to imbibe
Than what their reason, and their sense prescribe, –
That is, themselves; for what a man calls his,
In such a case, is really what he is.[27]

The individual's reliance on his own reason is thus interpreted as an expression of egotistic solipsism. And the point is made even more clearly in the brief gnomic lyric, "The Self-Subordination of Reason":

My Reason is I, and your Reason is You,
And if we shall differ, both cannot be true;
If Reason must judge, and we two must agree,
Another, third Reason must give the decree.[28]

Byrom's strictures on the subjectivity of reason have some affinity with the ideas of Prior and Blake.

[25] *Ibid.*, II, 194 (lines 315–16, 320–4).
[26] *Appeal to All that Doubt*, Law, VI, 72.
[27] Lines 969–72, *Poems*, II, 244. Conyers Middleton (1683–1750) was a clergyman whose *Discourses on Miracles* (1747–8) forestalled Hume's essay on the same subject (1748), and, it is said, provoked Gibbon into becoming a Roman Catholic. In 1750 he published a rejoinder to Sherlock's work on prophecy.
[28] *Poems*, I, 569.

Prior was sceptical enough to pour cold water on the mighty Locke, on the grounds that he was "a metaphysician running in a circle after his own understanding ... like a dog endeavouring to catch his own tail."[29] Prior indeed verges on solipsism in his vision of the subjectivity of human reason, and seeks to demolish Locke by claiming that "if no man's ideas be perfectly the same Locke's Human Understanding may be fit only for the meditation of Locke himself."[30] Byrom would have concurred with this element in Prior's scepticism. He would likewise have welcomed Blake's contribution to the argument. This is couched in the form of a gnomic lyric and contains strong echoes of Byrom's own definition of the subjectivity of human reason. In Blake's words:

> The vision of Christ that thou dost see
> Is my vision's greatest enemy:
> Thine has a great hook nose like thine,
> Mine has a snub nose like to mine:
> . . . .
> Both read the Bible day and night
> But thou readst black where I read white.[31]

The way out of this dilemma for Byrom and Blake is to develop, on the grounds of subjectivity, a theory of spirit, vision, or imagination.

It thus becomes necessary for Byrom to distinguish between two orders of truth, on the one hand the axiomatic truths and assumptions of the Enlightenment, which provoke a common response in the external reason of each man, and on the other, those deeper insights which depend on the quality of the internal reason of each man:

> In truths that nobody can miss,
> It is the Quid that makes the Quis;
> In such as lie more deeply hid,
> It is the Quis that makes the Quid.[32]

In the latter case it is the subjective reason which determines the quality of the truth, whereas in the former the external truth determines the automatic assent of the understanding. Byrom himself draws the conclusion in terms which match those of Law's analogy between imagination and God:

[29] "Locke and Montaigne" (1721), Prior, I, 625.
[30] *Ibid.*, I, 638.
[31] "The Everlasting Gospel" (c. 1818), in William Blake, *Poetry and Prose*, ed. G. Keynes (London: Nonesuch Press, 1956), p. 133.
[32] "The Quid and the Quis," *Poems*, I, 569.

We had much talk about reason, enthu., and I parted from him saying, No reason but the Logos = J.C., that reason was nothing if it was but a grammatical term and different in every man, but the true Reason was the Logos Jesus Christ.[33]

Once again this distinction between the two reasons is precisely that insisted upon by Coleridge.

The third way in which Law in particular supports the existence of an inward ground, or imagination, is by interpreting as metaphysical realities the microcosmic correspondences of the previous century. He derives these in a particularly purist form from Boehme. In perpetuating this pre-Enlightenment structure, Law was being patently reactionary. But, seen in the light of his interpretation of Newton, the structure does not stand or fall as a scientific hypothesis. It is presented rather as a metaphysic, designed to buttress an interpretation of human nature which includes the phenomena of man's relation to God and the world. It is in this light that one can most usefully consider Law's reliance on microcosmic correspondences.

Man is a little world because "Nature within and without man is one and the same, and has but one and the same way of working; a stone in the body and a stone out of the body of man proceeds from one and the same disorder of Nature."[34] And man needs the light and spirit of God, just as nature needs the light and spirit of the world:

For every perfect fruit openly declares, that it can have no goodness in it, till the light and spirit of this world has done that to it and in it, which the light and spirit of God must do to the soul of man, and therefore is a full proof, that it is as absolutely necessary for every human creature to desire, believe and receive the birth of the Son and Holy Spirit of God to save it from its own wrath and darkness, as it is necessary for every fruit of the earth to be raised and regenerated from its own bitterness and sourness by receiving the light and spirit of this world into it.[35]

The argument from correspondences begins to appear as a refutation of Cartesian dualism and a return to a full humanism wherein nature is interpreted in moral terms. Good and evil are not abstractions outside the fabric of nature; nor therefore are angels and devils. Man's nature is the ground in which these apparent abstractions are planted:

The same strong desire, fiery wrath, and stinging motion is in Holy Angels, that is in Devils, just as the same sourness, astringency, and biting bitter-

[33] Diary, 22 May 1736, *Remains*, II, 48.
[34] *Appeal to All Who Doubt*, Law, VI, 66.
[35] *Ibid.*, VI, 85.

ness, is in full ripened fruit, which was there before it received the riches of the light and spirit of the air. In a ripened fruit, its first sourness, astringency and bitterness, is not lost, nor destroyed, but becomes the real cause of all its rich spirit, fine taste, fragrant smell and beautiful colour.[36]

Law's argument carries the seeds of revolutionary heresy; in spite of its obscurantist tinge, it is designed to convey the same insights into the nature of man as those which characterise the Metaphysical poets and Blake.

Thus Herbert, in a world where resemblances and correspondences were not threatened by Cartesian dualism, could write of "Virtue" which "like seasoned timber never gives." And Blake, in a single-handed attempt to revive the aesthetic implications of Paracelsus and Boehme, laid the ground for his own poetic vision in terms which closely follow those of Law's argument.[37] Law's "wrath" is Blake's "energy"; hence Blake's "Tiger." For Law, as for Blake, "without contraries is no progression. Attraction and repulsion, reason and energy, love and hate, are necessary to human existence."[38] Law would have agreed with Blake's attack on the static dualism of orthodox religion, according to which "energy, called evil, is alone from the body; and ... reason, called good, is alone from the soul."[39] And from Law's dynamic theory of the little world of man, there is but a short step to Blake's own formula that "energy is the only life and is from the body; and reason is the bound or outward circumference of energy."[40] It is fair to say that in Law's system, once light and spirit have worked on desire and wrath, then "energy is eternal delight."[41]

The fourth stage in Law's definition of the imagination or inward ground can be deduced from the third. Law used the theory of

[36] *Ibid.*, VI, 70.

[37] See in particular "The Marriage of Heaven and Hell" (c. 1793). Note that in this work Blake sets a high value on the writings of Boehme and Paracelsus, and describes the work of his first master, Swedenborg, as derivative. Blake, pp. 190–1. Cf. Hobhouse's observation that "Divine Imagination (J. B.'s actual word) plays almost as important a part in his drama of the universe as it does in William Blake's, where it appears at times as the one great reality, the saviour of the world, uniting nature and spirit." Hans L. Martensen, *Jacob Boehme*, ed. S. Hobhouse (London: Rockliff, 1949), p. 43. Martensen's book was originally published in Danish in 1882.

[38] Blake, p. 181. Cf. Hobhouse, who glosses Boehme's "In Ja und Nein bestehen alle dinge – In Yes and No all things consist" as follows: "This is the root idea behind Blake's *Marriage of Heaven and Hell*; ... For J. B. and Blake, hell is the hidden foundation of heaven; wrath and evil (when hidden) that of love and good; 'without contraries there is no progression'." Martensen, p. 45.

[39] Blake, p. 182.

[40] *Ibid.*

[41] *Ibid.*

microcosmic correspondences to support his argument for the organic reality of nature. To circumvent the difficulties raised by Cartesian dualism, it follows that Law must argue for the spirituality of matter. In the Cartesian system of things spirituality had been forced into the tight corner of Malebranchian occasionalism. Law sought to define a revolutionary alternative as follows: "Body and spirit are not two separate independent things, but are necessary to each other, and are only the inward and outward conditions of one and the same being."[42] This formula has unmistakable affinities with that advanced by Blake in "The Marriage of Heaven and Hell." Blake attacked the proposition "that man has two real existing principles: viz: a body and a soul." According to him, "man has no body distinct from his soul; for that called body is a portion of soul discerned by the five senses, the chief inlets of soul in this age."[43] If Blake was misunderstood in his age, it is hardly surprising that Law, writing in the middle of the 18th century, had problems of communication.

To those for whom his *Spirit of Love* was unadulterated nonsense, Law spelled out his own interpretation of 18th century assumptions:

> Nay, if you was to say, that God first creates a soul out of nothing, and when that is done, then takes an understanding faculty, and puts it into it, after that a will, and then a memory, all as independently made as when a tailor first makes the body of a coat, and then adds sleeves or pockets to it; was you to say this, the schools of Descartes, Malebranche, or Locke could have nothing to say against it.[44]

Philosophically this may be a facile resort to Platonism, but as a cultural phenomenon in mid-18th century England, it represents a discovery with revolutionary aesthetic implications and an argument which was to be significantly developed by Blake and Coleridge.

Law of course had theological reasons for wanting to identify matter and spirit, and he drew up his theological argument for the spirituality of matter in no uncertain way:

> Now the reason, why there are spiritual properties in all the material things of this world, is only this, it is because the matter of this world is the materiality of the Kingdom of Heaven brought down into a created state of grossness, death and imprisonment... These heavenly properties

[42] *Spirit of Love*, Law, VIII, 16. Cf. Martensen's distinction between Boehme and the mystical tradition: "While mysticism excludes from the being of God the faintest trace of corporeity, demanding that all symbolical images must be swept far from God, ... Boehme teaches an eternal nature in God, and ascribes to God Fancy, or, as he terms it,Imagination." Martensen, p. 29.

[43] Blake, p. 182.

[44] Law, VIII, 31.

> ... lie in a continual desire to return to their first state of glory; and this is the groaning of the whole Creation to be delivered from vanity, which the Apostle speaks of... Quench this desire, and suppose there is nothing in the matter of this world that desires to be restored to its first glory, and then all the breaking forth of fire, light, brightness and glance in the things of this world, is utterly quenched with it.[45]

On the face of it, this is mystical Platonic theology; but even here the language ("fire, light, brightness and glance") and the structure of thought indicate clear sources of an aesthetic radically different from those preromantic tendencies which were conditioned by the theories of Descartes, Malebranche and Locke.

Law developed these aesthetic implications in the context of his spiritual insight. In so doing, he not only recalls the rhetoric and ideology of Donne's passage on the bell that tolls for every man, but also anticipates the whole range of Romantic theory concerning the spiritual significance of the least material phenomenon, whether this be expressed as Wordsworthian communion, Joycean epiphany, or Lawrentian symbolism:

> The materiality of this world is come out of a higher, and spiritual state, because every matter upon earth can be made to discover spiritual properties concealed in it... So that every time you see a piece of matter dissolved by fire, you have a full proof, that all the materiality of this world is appointed to a dissolution by fire; and that then, (O glorious day!) sun and stars, and all the elements will be delivered from vanity, will be again that one eternal, harmonious, glorious thing, which they were, before they were compacted into material distinctions and separations.[46]

The structure of Law's argument may be couched in obscurantism, but the vision that this structure supports is undoubtedly at variance with the spirit of the age; it reaches backwards to the spirit of Donne, and forwards to the spirit of Blake.

[45] *Appeal to All that Doubt*, Law, VI, 134.
[46] *Ibid.*, VI, 118.

CONCLUSION

It will by now be clear that a claim is being made on behalf of Ken, Byrom and Law which is not commensurate with their adducible literary merit. To the positivist literary critic this claim may sound like a piece of special pleading, but it can be argued that positivist criticism has its pitfalls and that one of its limitations is its failure to do justice to the relativism of aesthetics, to inter-disciplinary connections, and to the developmental approach which demands an appraisal of the potential as well as the actual in a given cultural product.

A positivist approach to Ken will perhaps come up with the descriptive judgment of "a green spot" (Keble) or "a green oasis" (Fairchild). Some might consider even these conclusions over-generous. When we come to the most generous appraisal of Byrom that is available, we are bound to question whether it does not owe more to ideological prejudice than to aesthetic judgment. Thus John Wesley wrote:

> In my journey from Liverpool I read Dr Byrom's poems. He has all the wit and humour of Dr Swift, together with much more learning, and deep and strong understanding, and, above all, a serious vein of piety... A few things in the second volume are taken from Jacob Behmen; to whom I object... But, setting these things aside, we have some of the finest sentiments that ever appeared in the English tongue; some of the noblest truths, expressed with the utmost energy of language, and the strongest colours of poetry.[1]

Wesley probably read Byrom on horseback and his praise must seem absurdly erratic on strictly aesthetic grounds. As a document of cultural history, as evidence of a certain kind of Augustan taste, less iconoclastic than one would perhaps expect, Wesley's judgment is illuminating.

[1] *Journal* (12 July 1773), John Wesley, *Works* (14 vols.; Grand Rapids, Michigan: Zondervan, 1958–9), III, 502–3. Quoted in Overton, p. 362 and in Baker, p. 61.

The modern critic will perhaps be happier with Wesley's parallel encomium on Law. It declares that there are "few writers in the present age who stand in any competition with Mr Law, as to beauty and strength of language; readiness, liveliness, and copiousness of thought; and (in many points) accuracy of sentiment." Wesley adds that several of Law's treatises "must remain, as long as England stands, almost unequalled standards of the strength and purity of our language, as well as of sound practical divinity."[2] The strength and purity of Law's language has undoubtedly been neglected, but it could probably be agreed that Law has his place between Swift and Gibbon in the golden age of English prose.

And yet Law as literature is like the Bible as literature; his real stature is thereby diminished. What we have chosen to insist on is that quality in Law's prose which is inseparable from his philosophy or vision of life, and which has led Henri Talon, if no one else, to the conclusion that Law was a "potential poet."[3] At times this poetic quality comes to the surface in a striking manner. What after all is one to make of the brief sentence Talon extracts from one of Law's pages – "In every man ... there is a dark guest ... lulled asleep by worldly light." – ?[4] Talon at least does some justice to Law in claiming that his "thought is not merely conceptual but sensory, as it may well

[2] Quoted in Christopher Walton, *Notes and Materials for an adequate Biography of the Celebrated Divine and Theosopher William Law* (London: privately printed, 1854), p. 564. Quoted on Walton's authority by Overton, p. 384 and Baker, p. 47. This encomium of Law's literary qualities comes from Wesley's preface to his devastating attack on Law's ideas in the famous letter of January 1756. Strangely enough this preface is not printed in either Wesley's *Works* or in Telford's edition of Wesley's letters.

[3] Talon, *William Law*, p. 89.

[4] *Ibid.*, p. 88. Talon, to make his point, has abbreviated Law drastically. Law actually wrote:

"Who has not at one time or other felt a sourness, wrath, selfishness, envy, and pride, which he could not tell what to do with, or how to bear, rising up in him without his consent, casting a blackness over all his thoughts, and then as suddenly going off again, either by the cheerfulness of the sun, or air, or some agreable accident, and again at times as suddenly returning upon him? Sufficient indications are these to every man that there is a dark guest within him, concealed under the cover of flesh and blood, often lulled asleep by worldly light and amusements, yet such as will, in spite of everything, show itself, which if it has not its proper relief in this life, must be his torment in eternity. And it was for the sake of this hidden hell within us, that our Blessed Lord said when on earth, and says now to every soul, 'Come unto me, all ye that labour and are heavy laden, and I will give you rest'."

The Grounds and Reasons of Christian Regeneration (1739), Law, V, 141. Here it is clear that the poetic quintessence extracted by Talon is part and parcel of a coherent structure of thought and moral vision which is itself potentially poetic.

On the purely technical structure of Law's prose, cf. F. D. Maurice's judgment (1844) that "Law is the most *continuous* writer in our language, each of his sentences and paragraphs leading on naturally, and as it were necessarily, to that which follows." Quoted in Baker, p. vii. Maurice concludes that to quote Law is virtually impossible.

be in a man who believed that the spirit reveals itself through its body."[5] What we have tried to show is that such distillation of poetic beauty is the outward and visible sign of a coherent whole.

This is the kind of perspective in which Law's work, and Byrom's reflection of it, together with Ken's before them, make for profitable reading. For it is at this level that they reveal not only their own limitations but also the lineaments of Augustan culture as it waxed and waned against certain radical alternatives.

[5] Talon, *William Law*, p. 88.

APPENDIX I

KEN'S HEROIC DIVINES[1]

Henry Hammond (1605–60), divine and Biblical critic, was chaplain to the Royal Commissioners at the abortive Uxbridge Conference (1645) where he disputed fruitlessly with the Parliamentary Presbyterians. Ken presumably refers to Hammond's *Mysterium Religionis, an Expedient for the composing Differences of Religion* (1649). Hammond would have become Bishop of Worcester had he lived.

John Gauden (1605–62), Bishop of Worcester, displayed Parliamentary sympathies from 1640. Believing that episcopacy needed reform but not abolition, he wrote against the execution of Charles I but retained his preferments during the Interregnum. Ken refers to his attempts in 1656 to promote agreement between Presbyterians and Episcopalians on the basis of Archbishop Ussher's model, and perhaps also to his *Hieraspistes: A Defence by way of Apology for the Ministry and Ministers of the Church of England* (1653) and his *Petitionary Remonstrance* (1659) on behalf of the deprived clergy.

Jeremy Taylor (1613–67), Bishop of Down and Connor, had the unenvious task of winning over the Presbyterian ministers of Ulster to the episcopal cause. He failed conspicuously and, "intending the reverse, did more than any man to establish the loyal Presbyterians of Ulster as a separate ecclesiastical body."

William Nicholson (1591–1672), Bishop of Gloucester, defended Anglican orthodoxy in pamphlets dated 1655 and 1659, and after the Restoration was conciliatory in his treatment of Dissenters, conniving at the preaching of those he respected.

Robert Sanderson (1587–1663), Bishop of Lincoln and Professor of Divinity at Oxford, was compelled to revise the forms of Common Prayer to appease the Parliamentarians in his neighbourhood. He came to the defence of Anglicanism with his *De Juramento* (1655) and *De Obligatione Conscientiae* (1660), and acted as Moderator at the 1661 conference of Presbyterian divines.

James Ussher (1581–1656), Archbishop of Armagh, was the author of a modified scheme of episcopacy. This was presented to a parliamentary sub-committee in 1641 and published in 1656 as *The Reduction of Episcopacy*

[1] See p. 52.

unto the form of Synodical Government received in the Ancient Church. It was widely accepted by Puritan leaders and used by Charles II as the basis of his 1660 Declaration. In 1655 Ussher approached Cromwell with a request that episcopal clergy be allowed to minister in private.

Joseph Hall (1574–1656), Bishop of Norwich, whose youthful satires (1597) were ordered to be burnt by Archbishop Whitgift, sat on the 1641 parliamentary committee along with Ussher as a moderate. *DNB*

APPENDIX II

LIST OF WILLIAM LAW'S WORKS

1. *Three Letters to the Bishop of Bangor* (1717–19)
2. *Remarks upon the Fable of the Bees* (1724)
3. *The Absolute Unlawfulness of the Stage Entertainment fully demonstrated* (1726)
4. *A Practical Treatise upon Christian Perfection* (1726)
5. *A Serious Call to a Devout and Holy Life* (1728)
6. *The Case of Reason, or Natural Religion fairly and fully Stated in Answer to Christianity as Old as the Creation* (1731)
7. *A Demonstration of the Gross and Fundamental Errors of* [Hoadly's] ... *'Plain Account of the Lord's Supper'* (1737)
8. *The Grounds and Reasons of the Christian Regeneration* (1739)
9. *An Earnest and Serious Answer to Dr Trapp's Discourse of the Folly, Sin, and Danger of being Righteous Overmuch* (1740)
10. *An Appeal to All that Doubt or Disbelieve the Truths of the Gospel, to which are added Some Animadversions upon Dr Trapp's Replies* (1740)
11. *The Spirit of Prayer* (1749)
12. *The Way to Divine Knowledge* (1752)
13. *The Spirit of Love* (1752–4)
14. *A Short but Sufficient Confutation of the Rev. Dr Warburton's projected defence (as he calls it) of Christianity* (1757)
15. *Of Justification by Faith and Works: a Dialogue between a Methodist and a Churchman* (1760)
16. *A Collection of Letters* (1760)
17. *An Humble, Earnest, and Affectionate Address to the Clergy* (1761)
18. *Letters to a Lady inclined to join the Church of Rome* (1779, written 1731–2)

BIBLIOGRAPHY

I. KEN, BYROM AND LAW: PRIMARY TEXTS

Byrom, John. *Private Journal and Literary Remains*. Edited by Richard Parkinson. 2 vols., issued in 4 parts. "Chetham Society Remains," Vols. 32, 34, 40, 44. Manchester: Chetham Society, 1854–7.

— *Poems*. Edited by A. W. Ward. 3 vols., issued in 5 parts. "Chetham Society Remains, New Series," Vols. 29, 30, 34, 35, 70. Manchester: Chetham Society, 1894–1912.

Ken, Thomas. *Works*. Edited by William Hawkins. 4 vols. London: V. Wyat, 1721.

— *The Prose Works*. Edited by W. Benham. London: Griffith, Farran, Okeden and Welsh, 1889.

Law, William. *Works*. Edited by G. B. Morgan. 9 vols. Brockenhurst and Canterbury: privately printed for G. Moreton, 1892–3.

2. KEN, BYROM AND LAW: SECONDARY TEXTS

Anderdon, John Lavicount. *The Life of Thomas Ken. By a Layman*. 2nd ed. revised and enlarged. London, 1854.

Baker, Eric W. *A Herald of the Evangelical Revival. A Critical Inquiry into the Relation of William Law to John Wesley and the Beginnings of Methodism*. London: Epworth Press, 1948.

Green, J. Brazier. *John Wesley and William Law*. London: Epworth Press, 1945.

Hawkins, William. *A Short Account of T. Ken D.D.* London: J. Wyat, 1713.

Hobhouse, Stephen Henry. *William Law and 18th Century Quakerism*. London: Allen and Unwin, 1927.

— *Selected Mystical Writings of William Law. With Studies in the Mystical Theology of William Law and Jacob Boehme, and an Inquiry into the Influence of Jacob Boehme on Isaac Newton*. 2nd ed. revised. London: Rockliff, 1948.

Overton, John Henry. *William Law, Nonjuror and Mystic*. London: Longmans, 1881.

Plumptre, Edward Hayes. *The Life of Thomas Ken, Bishop of Bath and Wells*. 2 vols. London: W. Isbister, 1888.

Rice, H. A. L. *Thomas Ken: Bishop and Non-Juror*. London: Society for the Propagation of Christian Knowledge, 1958.

Spurgeon, Caroline Frances Eleanor. "William Law and the Mystics," *Cambridge History of English Literature* (edited by A. W. Ward and A. R. Waller), IX (1912), 305–28.

Stephen, Leslie. "John Byrom," *Studies of a Biographer* (London: Smith Elder, 1907), I, 69–97.

Talon, Henri. *William Law. A Study in Literary Craftsmanship*. London: Rockliff, 1948.

— (ed.)) *Selections from the Journals and Papers of John Byrom, with Notes and Biographical Sketches of some of his Notable Contemporaries*. London: Rockliff, 1951.

Tighe, Richard. *A Short Account of the Life and Writings of the late Rev. William Law, A.M. with an Appendix, which contains Specimens of the Writings*. London: J. Hatchard and Elizabeth Budd, 1813.

Walton, Christopher. *Notes and Materials for an Adequate Biography of the Celebrated Divine and Theosopher William Law*. London: privately printed, 1854.

Whyte, Alexander. *Characters and Characteristics of William Law, Nonjuror and Mystic*. London: Hodder and Stoughton, 1893.

3. OTHER PRIMARY TEXTS

Aubrey, John. *Brief Lives*. Edited by Andrew Clark. 2 vols. Oxford: Clarendon Press, 1898.

Berkeley, George. *Alciphron*. Edited by T. E. Jessop. London: Thomas Nelson, 1950.

Blake, William. *Poetry and Prose*. Edited by Geoffrey Keynes. London: Nonesuch Press, 1956.

Boehme, Jacob. *The Signature of All Things*. London: J. M. Dent, 1912.

Bossuet, Jacques Bénigne. *Quakerism à la Mode: or A History of Quietism particularly that of the Lord Archbishop of Cambray and Madame Guyone. Done into English*. London: J. Harris and A. Bell, 1698.

Burnet, Gilbert. *History of My Own Time*. Edited by Osmund Airy. 2 vols: Oxford: Clarendon Press, 1897–1900.

Butler, Joseph. *Works*. Edited by W. E. Gladstone. 2 vols. Oxford: Clarendon Press, 1897.

Chalmers, Alexander (ed.). *The Works of the English Poets from Chaucer to Cowper*. 21 vols. London: J. Johnson, 1810.

Coleridge, Samuel Taylor. *Biographia Literaria*. Edited by Arthur Symons. London: J. M. Dent, 1906.

— *On the 17th Century*. Edited by Roberta Florence Brinkley. Durham, North Carolina: Duke University Press, 1955.

Collins, Anthony. *A Discourse of Freethinking*. London, 1713.

Donne, John. *Complete Poems and Selected Prose*. Edited by John Hayward. London: Nonesuch Press, 1955.

Dryden, John. *Poems*. Edited by John Sargeaunt. London: Oxford University Press, 1910.

Dunton, John. *Life and Errors*. Edited by J. B. Nichols. London, 1818.

Fénelon (François de Salignac de la Mothe). *De l'existence et des attributs de Dieu*. Paris: Didot, 1853.

Herbert, George. *Works*. Edited by F. E. Hutchinson. Oxford: Clarendon Press, 1945.

Hervey, James. *Works*. Newcastle: M. Brown, 1789.

Johnson, Samuel. *A Dictionary of the English Language*. 2 vols. 6th ed. London: Rivington, 1785.

Lead, Jane. *A Fountain of Gardens*. Edited by Francis Lee. 3 vols. London, 1697–1701.

Lee, Henry. *Anti-Scepticism: or Notes upon Each Chapter of Locke's Essay*. London, 1702.

Leland, John. *A View of the Principal Deistical Writers that have appeared in England in the last and present century, with observations upon them, and some account of the answers that have been published against them. In several letters to a friend*. 2 vols. 4th ed. London: Dodsley and Longman, 1764.

Leslie, Charles. *The Snake in the Grass: or Satan Transformed into an Angel of Light*. 3rd ed. London: Charles Brome, 1698.

Locke, John. *Works*. 9 vols. 12th ed. London: Rivington, 1824.

Mandeville, Bernard de. *A Letter to Dion*. Edited by J. Viner. "Augustan Reprint Society," No. 41. Los Angeles: University of California Press, 1953.

Marvell, Andrew. *Poems and Letters*. Edited by H. M. Margoliouth. 2 vols. Oxford: Clarendon Press, 1927.

More, Paul Elmer, and Cross, Frank Leslie (ed.). *Anglicanism*. London: Society for the Propagation of Christian Knowledge, 1935.

Pope, Alexander. *Poems*. Edited by John Butt. London: Methuen, 1963.

Prior, Matthew. *The Literary Works*. Edited by H. Bunker Wright and Monroe K. Spears. 2 vols. Oxford: Clarendon Press, 1959.

Ray, John. *The Wisdom of God Manifested in the Works of the Creation*. London, 1691.

Selby-Bigge, L. A. (ed.). *British Moralists: being Selections from Writers principally of the 18th Century*. 2 vols. Oxford: Clarendon Press, 1897.

Swift, Jonathan. *Works*. Edited by Herbert Davis. 14 vols. Oxford: Blackwell, 1939–62.

Tillotson, John. *Works*. Edited by Thomas Birch. 10 vols. London: Richard Priestly, 1820.

Tindal, Matthew. *Christianity as Old as the Creation, or the Gospel a Republication of the Religion of Nature*. London, 1730.

Toland, John. *Christianity Not Mysterious*. London: Samuel Buckley, 1696.

Warburton, William. *Letters from a Late Eminent Prelate to one of his Friends*. 3rd ed. London: T. Cadell and W. Davies, 1809.

Watts, Isaac. *Works*. Edited by D. Jennings and P. Doddridge. 6 vols. London, 1753.

Wesley, John. *Works*. 14 vols. Grand Rapids, Michigan: Zondervan, 1958–9.

Winchilsea, Anne Finch, Countess of. *Poems*. Edited by Myra Reynolds. Chicago: University Press, 1903.

Wood, Anthony. *Life and Times*. Edited by Andrew Clark. 5 vols. "Oxford Historical Society." Oxford: Clarendon Press, 1891–1900.

Wordsworth, William. *The Poetical Works*. Edited by Thomas Hutchinson. Revised by Ernest de Selincourt. London: Oxford University Press, 1936.

4. OTHER SECONDARY TEXTS

Bronson, B. H. *Facets of the Enlightenment*. Berkeley and Los Angeles: University of California Press, 1968.

Broxap, Henry. *The Later Non-Jurors*. Cambridge: University Press, 1924.

Cassirer, Ernst. *The Philosophy of the Enlightenment*. Boston: Beacon Press, 1951.

Clarke, W. K. Lowther. *18th Century Piety*. London: Society for the Propagation of Christian Knowledge, 1945.

Colie, Rosalie. *Light and Enlightenment: A Study of the Cambridge Platonists and the Dutch Arminians*. Cambridge: University Press, 1957.

Cragg, Gerald Robertson. *From Puritanism to the Age of Reason: A Study of Changes in Religious Thought within the Church of England 1660–1700*. Cambridge: University Press, 1950.

Creed, John Martin, and Smith, John Sandwith Boys. *Religious Thought in the 18th Century, Illustrated from Writers of the Period*. Cambridge: University Press, 1934.

Cropper, Margaret Beatrice. *Flame Touches Flame*. London: Longmans Green, 1949.

— *Sparks Among the Stubble*. London: Longmans Green, 1955.

Eliot, T. S. *Selected Essays*. London: Faber and Faber, 1934.

Evans, Arthur William. *Warburton and the Warburtonians. A Study in Some 18th Century Controversies*. London: Oxford University Press, 1932.

Fairchild, Hoxie Neale. *Religious Trends in English Poetry*. 5 vols. New York: Columbia University Press, 1939–62.

Fussell, Paul. *The Rhetorical World of Augustan Humanism: Ethics and Imagery from Swift to Burke*. Oxford: Clarendon Press, 1965.

Greene, Donald. "Augustinianism and Empiricism: a Note on 18th Century English Intellectual History,"' *18th Century Studies*, I (1967), 33–68.

— *The Age of Exuberance*. New York: Random House, 1970.

Grierson, H. J. C. (ed.). *Metaphysical Lyrics and Poems of the 17th Century: Donne to Butler*. Oxford: Clarendon Press, 1921.

Hanzo, Thomas A. *Latitude and Restoration Criticism*. "Anglistica," No. 12. Copenhagen: Rosenkilde and Bagger, 1961.

Hawkins, L. M. *Allegiance in Church and State: The Problem of the Nonjurors in the English Revolution*. London: Routledge, 1928.

Hazard, Paul. *La crise de la conscience Européenne 1680–1715*. Paris: Boivin, 1935.

Henderson, P. A. Wright. *The Life and Times of John Wilkins*. Edinburgh: William Blackwood, 1910.

Hoyles, John. *The Waning of the Renaissance 1640–1740: Studies in the Thought and Poetry of Henry More, John Norris and Isaac Watts*. The Hague: Martinus Nijhoff, 1971.

Johnson, James. *The Formation of English Neoclassical Thought.* Princeton: University Press, 1967.

Keble, John. "Sacred Poetry," *The Quarterly Review*, XXXII (1825), 211–32.

Lawrence, D. H. *Women in Love.* London: Penguin Books, 1960.

Locke, Louis G. *Tillotson, A Study in 17th Century Literature.* "Anglistica," No. 4. Copenhagen: Rosenkilde and Bagger, 1954.

Macewen, Alexander Robertson. *Antoinette Bourignon, Quietist.* London: Hodder and Stoughton, 1910.

Martensen, Hans L. *Jacob Boehme.* Edited by Stephen Hobhouse. London: Rockliff, 1949.

Mossner, Ernest Campbell. *Bishop Butler and the Age of Reason: A Study in the History of Thought.* New York: Macmillan, 1936.

Orcibal, Jean. "The Theological Originality of John Wesley and Continental Spirituality," *A History of the Methodist Church in Great Britain* (edited by Rupert Davies and Gordon Rupp; London: Epworth Press, 1965), 83–111.

Osmond, Percy H. *The Mystical Poets of the English Church.* London: Society for the Propagation of Christian Knowledge, 1919.

Rodway, Allan. *The Romantic Conflict.* London: Chatto and Windus, 1963.

Rostvig, Maren-Sofie. *The Happy Man: Studies in the Metamorphoses of a Classical Ideal.* 2 vols. "Oslo Studies in English," Nos. 2 and 7. Oslo: Akademisk Forlag; Oxford: Blackwell, 1954–8.

Spurgeon, Caroline Frances Eleanor. *Mysticism in English Literature.* Cambridge: University Press, 1913.

Stephen, Leslie. *History of English Thought in the 18th Century.* 2 vols. London: Rupert Hart-Davis, 1962.

Stromberg, Roland Nelson. *Religious Liberalism in 18th Century England.* London: Oxford University Press, 1954.

Walton, Geoffrey. *Metaphysical to Augustan: Studies in Tone and Sensibility in the 17th Century.* London: Bowes and Bowes, 1955.

Willey, Basil. *The 17th Century Background.* London: Penguin Books, 1962.

— *The 18th Century Background.* London: Penguin Books, 1962.

5. WORKS OF REFERENCE

Diccionario de Filosofia. Buenos Aires, 1958.

Dictionary of American Biography. New York, 1928–37. (= *DAB*)

Dictionary of National Biography. London, 1885–1901. (= *DNB*)

Enciclopedia Filosofica. Venezia-Rome, 1957.

New Catholic Encyclopaedia. New York, 1967.

Oxford English Dictionary. Oxford, 1897–1928. (= *OED*)

Skeat, W. W. *An Etymological Dictionary of the English Language.* Oxford: Clarendon Press, 1910.

INDEX